Acts 1-12

"The Church Is Born"

#Ac1-NK-SS

A Bible-Based Study

For Individuals and Groups

Leader's Guide Included

5/13
Turn to.
me & I will
heal your
land

Lamplighters International
St. Louis Park, Minnesota, USA 55416
www.LamplightersUSA.org

Sixth Printing – June 2010

Lamplighters International
St. Louis Park, Minnesota USA 55416

Lamplighters International is a ministry that publishes Christ-centered, Bible-based teaching discipleship resources.

For additional information about the Lamplighters ministry resources contact:
Lamplighters International 6301 Wayzata Blvd, St. Louis Park, Minnesota USA 55416 or visit our web site at www.LamplightersUSA.org.

ISBN # 1-931372-14-4
Order # Ac1-NK-SS

Contents

How to Use This Bible Study

What is Lamplighters?

Lamplighters is a Christ-centered discipleship ministry that is designed to increase your understanding of God's Word and equip you to serve Him more effectively. Each Lamplighters Bible Study is a self-contained unit and an integral part of the entire discipleship ministry.

This study is comprised of five or ten individual lessons, depending on the format you choose. When you have completed the entire study you will have a much greater understanding of a significant portion of God's Word. You will also have learned several new truths that you can apply to your life.

How to Study a Lamplighters Lesson.

A Lamplighters study begins with prayer, your Bible, the weekly lesson, and a sincere desire to learn more about God's Word. The questions are presented in a progressive sequence as you work through the study material. You should not use Bible commentaries or other reference books until you have completed your weekly lesson and met with your weekly group. When you approach the Bible study in this way, you will have the opportunity to personally discover many valuable spiritual truths from the Word of God.

As you prepare for your lesson, find a quiet place to complete your weekly lesson. Each study (Part "a" or "b") will take approximately thirty minutes to complete. If you are new to Lamplighters materials, you should plan to spend more time on the first few lessons. Your weekly personal study time will decrease as you become familiar with the format. Soon you will look forward each week to discovering important life principles in the coming lessons.

You should write your answers in your own words in the space provided within the weekly studies. We have intentionally provided a significant amount of writing space for this purpose. Include appropriate verse references at the end of your carefully worded and thoughtful answers, unless the question calls for a personal opinion. The answers to the questions will be found in the Scripture references at the end of the questions or in the passages listed at the beginning of each study.

"*Do you think*" Questions

Each weekly study has a few "*do you think*" questions. These questions ask you to make personal applications from the Biblical truths you are learning. Make a special effort to answer these questions because they are designed to help you apply God's Word to your life. In the first two lessons the "*do you think*" questions are placed in italic print for easy identification. If you are part of a study group, your insightful answers to these questions could be a great source of spiritual encouragement to others.

How to Use This Study Guide

The Lamplighters discipleship materials are designed for a variety of ministry applications. They have been used successfully in the following settings:

Self-study - Read the passage listed at the beginning of the weekly lesson. Seek to gain as much understanding from the Text as possible. Answer the questions in the space provided, using complete sentences if the space allows. Complete the entire lesson without looking at the Leader's Guide in the back of the book. Discipline yourself to answer all the questions so that you gain the maximum benefit from the lesson. When you have completed the lesson, read the corresponding portion of the Leader's Guide to gain greater understanding of the passage you have just studied.

One-on-one discipleship - Complete the entire lesson without referring to the Leader's Guide. If you are leading the one-on-one discipleship time meeting, become familiar with the Leader's Guide answers before you meet with the person you are discipling. Plan to meet for approximately one hour to discuss the lesson. If you are not the leader, do not look at the Leader's Guide until you have met for the meeting.

Small Group discipleship - The members of the discipleship group should complete their weekly lessons without referring to the Leader's Guide. The Group Leader should complete the lesson before he becomes thoroughly familiar with the Leader's Guide answers. A comprehensive ministry manual has been prepared for church leaders to help lead small groups effectively and implement the Lamplighters discipleship ministry into their church.

Class teaching (Adult or Senior High Sunday School Classes) - The pastor or teacher should complete the entire lesson before class, review the Leader's Guide answers, and prayerfully consider how to present the lesson. The class members should complete their weekly lessons in advance so that they can bring their thoughtful insights and questions to the class discussion time. The Teacher's Edition makes an excellent companion to this format and allows the teacher to design specific lessons appropriate in length and knowledge level for the students. For more information on combining these two products, contact Lamplighters or visit our website

Personal Questions

Occasionally you will be asked to respond to personal questions that you should do your best to answer. If you are part of a study group, you will not be asked to share any personal information about yourself. However, be sure to answer these questions for your own benefit because they will help you compare your present level of spiritual maturity to the Biblical principles presented in the lesson.

A Final Word

Throughout this study the masculine pronouns are often used in the generic sense to avoid awkward sentence construction. When the pronouns "he," "him," and "his" are used to refer to the Trinity (God the father, Jesus Christ and the Holy Spirit), they always refer to the masculine gender.

This Lamplighters study is presented after many hours of careful preparation. It is our prayer that it will help you **grow in the grace and knowledge of our Lord and Savior Jesus Christ. To Him be the glory both now and forever. Amen** (2 Peter 3:18).

About the Author

John Alexander Stewart was born and raised near Winnipeg, Canada. He was drafted by the Pittsburgh Penguins (NHL) and played professional hockey for eight years. He was born again in 1977 when he accepted Jesus Christ alone for eternal life. He graduated from seminary in 1988. He served as a pastor for fifteen years. During this time he planted two Bible-believing churches. He also founded Lamplighters International and now serves as the executive director of the ministry.

Study #1a   You Shall Be My Witnesses

Read - Introduction, Acts 1:1-2:47; other references as given.

The book of Acts is the sequel to the third gospel, both written by Luke, the beloved physician and missionary. Both books are addressed to a man named Theophilus whose name means "a lover of God." For the past two thousand years, this book has inspired lovers of God. Empowered by the Spirit of God, the early church overcame government intrusion and persecution, hypocrisy, internal conflict, and the crippling cancer of religious traditionalism – perennial enemies of the church throughout the ages.

In this first study you will learn the difference between the kingdom of God and the church age. You will also learn four principles that will help you understand God's will for your life. Before you begin, take a moment to ask God to help you understand and apply the precious truths you will be learning. May God bless your study of His Word.

1. During the 40-day period between Christ's resurrection and ascension, He appeared to His followers many times (Acts 1:3). The Lord attested to the reality of His resurrection by many convincing proofs (Gr. *tekmeroin* - an infallible or indubitable proof, a powerful word used only once in the New Testament). He spoke specifically to His disciples concerning the kingdom of God. The term "kingdom of God" refers to the future time when Christ will rule personally on earth during the millennium kingdom (cf. Rev. 20:4).

    a. What question did the disciples keep asking Jesus Christ concerning the kingdom of God (Acts 1:6)?

    b. What did Jesus Christ say to His disciples concerning the kingdom of God (Acts. 1:7-8)?

2. Jesus said, **"You shall be witnesses to Me in Jerusalem, and in all Judea and Samaria, and to the end of the earth"** (Acts 1:8). Historically, the Christian church has understood Christ's words (often referred to as "The Great Commission") as His command to take the message of salvation to all nations. However, some interpret Christ's statement to be a simple statement of fact. (Note: The Greek language allows for both interpretations.)

a. How do we know that the disciples understood His statement to be a command to be obeyed rather than a simple statement of fact (Acts 4:17-20; 10:38-42)?

b. Take a moment to reflect upon your understanding of Christ's Great Commission (Acts 1:8). Do you believe it is a divine command to be obeyed or a simple statement of fact?

c. If you believe it is a command to be obeyed, what specific things are you doing to fulfill God's command to reach the world for Christ?

3. The "Great Commission" must have seemed like "Mission Impossible" to these eleven apostles who had denied Christ just days earlier (cf. Matt. 26:56; Jn. 18:25-27). What did Jesus say would enable them to fulfill His command (Acts 1:5, 8)?

4. Jesus redirected his disciples' thinking from the future kingdom of God to their present responsibility of being His witnesses. After that, He was lifted up from the Mount of Olives out of their sight (Acts 1:9, 12). Jehovah's Witnesses and other religious groups claim that Christ has already come back in spiritual form. What does the Bible teach about the final return of Jesus Christ to this earth (Acts 1:11; Zech. 14:1-4; Rev. 1:7; 19:11-19)?

5. The disciples returned a Sabbath day's journey (3/5ths of a mile) from the Mount of Olives to the upper room where they had previously held the Last Supper with Christ. In the upper room they devoted themselves to prayer (Acts 1:14). The specific phrase, **"with one accord"** (v. 14), is an important term that occurs two other times: once in Acts and once in Paul's letter to the Philippians.

a. What does it mean (Acts 2:46; 15:25; Phil. 1:27; 2:1-5)?

b.   What specific counsel would you give a Christian who had a problem being of one mind with another believer?

6.   According to Acts 1:18, Judas fell headlong and died. Matthew's gospel states that Judas hanged himself (cf. Matt. 27:5). How *do you think* this apparent inconsistency can be reconciled?

7.   Acts 1:15-26 focuses on the apostles' efforts to find a replacement for Judas. This Biblical passage seems insignificant to the development of the book, especially when Judas' replacement, Matthias, is never mentioned again in Scripture. However, this passage contains several essential principles on determining God's will for our lives – something believers of every generation need to understand.

a.   Peter addressed the group of about 120 people in the upper room (Acts 1:15). His words reveal the first principle (other than prayer) that God's people must employ if they expect to determine His will for their lives. What is this first principle (Acts 1:16-20a)?

b.   Peter's quotation of Psalm 109:8, **"Let another take his office"** reveals the second principle of determining God's will for their lives. What is it?

c.   Often Christians become confused when they have two legitimate choices that both seem within the will of God (e.g., the purchase of a home, selection of a college, etc.). What is the third principle to determine God's will (Acts 1:24)?

8.   **"The lot fell on Matthias. And he was numbered with the eleven apostles"** (Acts 1:26). The apostles responded to God's choice of Matthias as the twelfth apostle with the assurance of answered prayer. Sometimes God's people are plagued with second thoughts or doubts after making a decision. What is the fourth principle we need to incorporate when we seek to walk in God's will (Acts 1:26)?

Study #1b　　You Shall Be My Witnesses

Read - Acts 1:1-2:47; other references as given.

9.　On the day of Pentecost, **"they were all with one accord in one place"** (Acts 2:1), probably in the upper room or the temple court (cf. Acts 7:47). The Day of Pentecost (Gr. *pentekoste* - fiftieth day) was the name of the annual feast that occurred fifty days after Passover at the end of the Feast of Firstfruits (cf. Lev. 23:1-22). On Pentecost the Jews would bring offerings (i.e., firstfruits) at the beginning of the wheat harvest. What three significant things happened on this first Pentecost after Christ's ascension (Acts 2:1-4)?

10.　Pentecost was regarded as the anniversary of the giving of the Law to Moses on Mt. Sinai. The baptism with the Holy Spirit included a sound **"as of a rushing mighty wind"** and the appearance of **"tongues, as of fire"** resting on each one present (Acts 2:2-3). Both Greek words for *Spirit* and *wind* come from the same verb *pnoe,* which means "to blow" or "to breathe." The phrase **"as of a rushing mighty wind"** signifies the power of the Holy Spirit at His coming and His ability to infuse life into a body (i.e., the body of Christ, which is the church). The fulfillment of Christ's promise of the baptism with the Holy Spirit empowered the apostles to speak **"with other tongues"** (Gr. *dialektos* - discourse, tongue, conversation, language).

　　a.　Acts 2:3-13 is the only passage in the Bible that provides a definition of the Biblical gift of tongues. (Note: Other Biblical passages dealing with tongues merely mention its use or decry its misuse [Acts 10:46; 19:6; 1 Cor. 12-14].) Give a Biblical definition of the gift of tongues (Acts 2:4-13).

　　b.　How many times do the phrases **"in his own language"** or **"own tongues"** appear in Acts 2:4-13? Why do you think these phrases are emphasized in these few verses?

11.　Peter acted as the spokesman for the twelve apostles when he defended their actions before the multitude (Acts 2:14 ff.). His defense was based upon reason (Acts 2:15) and Scripture (Acts 2:16-21). Sometimes believers find it very difficult to know whether they should defend their actions before others. Some Christians even claim that a believer should never defend himself to others. What are some spiritual principles forth a believer to consider before he defends himself to other people (Pro. 15:1; 18:13; 26:4-5; 1 Cor. 10:31)?

12. Peter's sermon on the day of Pentecost defended the present actions of the apostles and attacked the past actions of those who killed Christ (Acts 2:22-36). Undoubtedly, many of the Jews were still confused about the exact identity of Jesus Christ. Peter's sermon answers three assumed questions: "If Jesus was really God, how could men have killed him?", "If Jesus was resurrected from the dead as the disciples claimed, where is He now?", and "If Jesus was resurrected, what is His present status in heaven and on earth?"

a. What did Peter say about Jesus the Nazarene prior to His death (Acts 2:22-23)?

b. What two things did Peter say about the death of Jesus Christ (Acts 2:23)?

c. How does Peter's explanation of the events of Jesus' death answer the question, "If Jesus was really God, how could men have killed him"?

d. What did Peter say about the resurrection of Jesus Christ (Acts 2:24)?

13. Although the resurrection of Jesus Christ is a fundamental of the Christian faith, some professing Christians consider it an optional doctrine. What did the apostle Paul say to the Corinthians about the resurrection (1 Cor. 15:12-19)?

14. How does Peter answer the second assumed question, "If Jesus was resurrected from the dead as the disciples claimed, where is He now"? (Acts 2:33)?

15. What is Peter's answer to the third assumed question, "If Jesus was resurrected, what is His present status in heaven and on earth?" (Acts 2:36)?

16. According to some evangelical standards, Peter's sermon would be too confrontational. His graphic statement **"you have taken by lawless hands, have crucified, and put to death"** (cf. Acts 2:23) laid the blame for Christ's death squarely at their feet. Peter is saying that even though the Jews used the hands of the godless men (i.e., the Romans - Pilate and his soldiers) to accomplish their wickedness, the ultimate responsibility for Christ's death belonged to them.

    a. How did the Jewish multitude initially respond to Peter's sermon (Acts 2:37)?

    b. How did Peter respond to their question (Acts 2:38-40)?

17. Three thousand people responded in faith to Peter's message and words of exhortation (Acts 2:41). They responded immediately to Christ by submitting to baptism (v. 41). They also continually devoted themselves to four essential aspects of healthy spiritual growth.

    a. What are they (Acts 2:42)?

    b. Take a few minutes to assess your relationship with Christ. Now examine the four aspects of healthy spiritual growth. Which one of these aspects do you need to focus upon to a greater degree?

18. The early church in Jerusalem was a model of healthy spiritual development. Rather than trying to manufacture ministry, they focused their attention on their relationship with God and let Him use them for His glory. List five positive spiritual by-products that occurred as a result of their devotion to Christ (Acts 2:43-47).

Study # 2a   The Power of Jesus' Name

Read – Acts 3:1-4:37; other references as given.

The church was born on the Day of Pentecost (Acts 2) when three thousand people were saved and baptized in one day. Can you imagine the scene—priests and tax collectors, men and women, nationals and foreigners—all repenting and coming together as one in Christ? No wonder the unsaved religious leaders said, **"By what power or by what name have you done this?"** (Acts 4:7).

In this lesson you will be learning how the early Jewish believers relied on the power of God alone to transform their culture. No gimmicks, no programs – just Jesus working in and through wholly devoted disciples. Before you begin, take a moment to ask God to help you understand and apply the precious truths you will be learning. May God bless your study of His Word.

1. Some days after Peter's sermon on the day of Pentecost, Peter and John went up to the temple to pray (Acts 3:1). The ancient Jerusalem temple stood on Mount Moriah, the same location where Abraham offered his son Isaac many years earlier (cf. Gen. 22:1-2). The Islamic Dome of the Rock, one of the three most sacred sites for the Moslem world, now stands on this sight.

    a. Today in Jerusalem, ultra-orthodox Jews walk silently to the Western or Wailing Wall with their heads bowed as they offer their daily prayers. (Note: The Western Wall is part of Herod's temple which was under construction during Jesus' day [cf. Jn. 2:18-20].). What happened as Peter and John were going up to the temple to pray (Acts 3:1-3)?

    b. The lame beggar's family and friends likely carried him up to the temple each day. Perhaps they even transported him to the temple twice daily for the morning and the evening sacrifices. Why do you think he went to the temple to beg (cf. De. 15:7-11; Acts 3:9)?

2. The lame beggar asked for alms but received physical healing instead (Acts 3:6, 7). The church of Jesus Christ has struggled throughout the centuries to understand its role as a benefactor to the poor. It has been said, "Feed a man a fish and you meet his need for a day, teach him how to fish and you meet his need for a lifetime, introduce him to the Great Fisherman and you meet his need for eternity." What basic spiritual principles should Christians remember when they consider their responsibility to the needy (Matt. 26:10-11; Gal. 2:9-10; 6:10)?

3.   In Acts 2, Luke mentioned that **"many wonders and signs were done through the apostles"** (cf. Acts 2:43). (**wonders**, Gr. *teras* – miracle; **signs**, Gr. *semeion* – sign, prodigy, a supernatural warning of a future event or God's authentic endorsement of one of His servants). In what way(s) do you think the healing of this man was both a wonder and a sign (Acts 3:2, 6-7)?

4.   The Book of Acts is not only a history of the early church but a detailed record of the infant church's struggle to understand God's plan for the church age. As you study the book notice that the early Christians were uncertain whether they should continue to adhere to the Old Covenant (i.e., the Law of Moses) or fully embrace the New Covenant way of life. What did Peter and John not understand when they went up to the temple to pray (Jn. 4:20-24; 1 Cor. 6:19)?

5.   The believer's ability to discern God's will and follow His plan is essential if he expects to be an effective servant of God. As a new creature in Christ, the Christian must learn to recognize and accept the need for Biblical change (cf. 2 Cor. 3:18; 5:17). If God's people resist all change, they will soon become spiritually obsolete, confusing man-made traditions with Biblical truth (cf. Mk. 7:1-13). If God's people innocently welcome all change, they will soon embrace the "wisdom of the world" and deny the Lord Jesus.

    a.   How well do you respond to change at home, ... at work, ... at church?

    b.   What could you and your church do to embrace Biblical change more without embracing the wisdom of the world that denies the Lord Jesus?

6.   The apostle Peter soon realized that the healed man and the other people believed that he had healed the beggar by his own authority (Acts 3:12). Although he could have used this situation to strengthen his influence over the people, he responded as a true servant of God.

    a.   What did Peter do or say to the people to help them understand that the true source of the man's healing was from God, not man (Acts 3:12-16)?

b. In what way(s) do you think you could apply Peter's example to various situations in your life?

7. In Peter's second sermon to the people (Acts 3:12-26), he emphasized three contradictions in the Jews' conduct during the trial of Jesus (Acts 3:13-15). First, he said the Jews demanded Christ's death even though Pilate wanted to release Him (v. 13). What were the last two contradictions that Peter identified (Acts 3:14-15)?

8. Again, Peter commanded the people to repent (Acts 3:19; cf. Acts 2:38). The word **repentance** (Gr. *metanoeo* – to change one's mind or thinking) emphasizes man's need to surrender his thoughts to the authority of God's Word. What specific truths did Peter want the people to accept …

a. about the healing of the lame beggar (Acts 3:16)?

b. about the suffering of Jesus Christ (Acts 3:18)?

c. about the consequences of their sin (Acts 3:19)?

9. Peter concludes his sermon with several references to the OT prophets (Acts 3:21-27). The Jews' love for Moses, Samuel, and the other prophets would have heightened their interest in his message. What did Moses and the other prophets say about Jesus that strengthened Peter's call for repentance (Acts 3:21-26)?

Study # 2b The Power of Jesus' Name

Before you begin, take a moment to ask God for His help as you study these precious truths in this passage.

10. The miraculous healing of the lame beggar was notable, but it was probably recorded in Scripture because of the negative reaction it caused among the religious leaders. After Peter concluded his message, the disciples continued to teach the listening crowd (Acts 4:1). While the disciples were teaching, the Jewish authorities confronted them for proclaiming the doctrine of the resurrection.

    a.   Give four reasons why their teaching of the resurrection was so disturbing to these religious leaders (Matt. 22:23; 28:12-15; Ro. 1:1-4; 1 Cor. 15:13-14)?

    b.   What did the religious leaders do in an attempt to prevent the disciples from teaching the resurrection (Acts 4:3-7)?

11. Shortly after the completion of Peter's second sermon, the church had already grown to more than 10,000, since the total number of believing men was now about five thousand. (Note: Some scholars believe the population of Jerusalem was about forty thousand at this time [Acts 4:4].)

    a.   What did Peter say to the Jewish authorities in response to their interrogation (Acts 4:8-10)?

b. Peter understood the extent of the political authority these religious leaders possessed. Nevertheless, he fearlessly reminded them that they were the ones who crucified Jesus and that God had raised Him from the dead (Acts 4:10). Christians often marvel at Peter's spiritual courage during this situation. Every believer possesses the same spiritual power to speak boldly in the name of Jesus. What is it (Acts 4:8)?

12. Many Christians are confused about the difference between the Spirit baptism and Spirit filling. Spirit baptism happens only once (i.e., at the time of salvation) and places the new believer into the body of Christ (cf. 1 Cor. 12:13). (Note: The notable exception of the timing was at the beginning of the church.) The believer is never commanded in Scripture to seek the baptism of the Holy Spirit. On the other hand the believer is commanded to seek the filling of the Spirit (cf. Eph. 5:18).

a. What do you think it means to **be filled with the Spirit** (Eph. 5:18)?

b. Are you seeking to be filled with the Spirit so that you can be a bold witness for Christ?

13. The Jewish authorities took Peter and John into custody, hoping to intimidate them and the new believers. However, when they observed the confidence of Peter and John, they eventually released them with a stern warning not to teach in this name. (Note: By this time the Jewish authorities did not want to even use Jesus' name [cf. Acts 4:4].). What did Peter say to the Jewish authorities when he and John were being released (Acts 4:19)?

14. When the apostles were released, they returned to the other believers and reported all that the chief priests and the elders had said to them (Acts 4:23). The believers lifted up their voices with one accord, thanking God for Jesus and expressing their

faith in God the Father (Acts 4:24-31). Some Christians find it difficult to maintain a joyful spirit when things are not going well for them. Most Christians find it nearly impossible to praise God during very difficult times. There are at least three reasons why these new believers were able to maintain genuine spiritual joy and a bold witness for Christ in the midst of persecution. What are they (Acts 4:24-31)?

15. When a believer is filled with the Spirit, he experiences a boldness to speak out about God (cf. Acts 2:11; 4:8). What else will be characteristic about a believer's life when he is filled with the Spirit (Acts 4:32-35)?

16. The phrase, **"Neither did anyone say that any of the things he possessed was his own, but they had all things in common"** has been used to endorse Christian communal living and even a Christianized form of communism (Acts 4:32). It has been said "Capitalism is the unequal distribution of wealth, socialism is the unequal distribution of poverty, and communism is socialism with a gun at your head.". Why is it a wrong use of Scripture to use this passage as an endorsement for Christian communal living or a Christianized form of communism (Acts 4:32-37; Phil. 2:14-15)?

Study # 3a   The Church's First Hypocrites

Read - Acts 5:1-6:7; other references as given.

In Biblical times the Greek word for hypocrite was used to refer to an actor who portrayed numerous characters in plays. The actor's true identity was hidden from the audience by the masks he wore. In this lesson you will learn how God dealt with the very first sin in the church: hypocrisy. You will also learn how prejudice and its consequences can threaten even the best churches.

Before you begin, take a moment to ask God to help you understand and apply the precious truths you will be learning. May God bless your study of His Word.

1. The first words in Acts 5, **"But a certain man ..."** introduce a comparison between the generosity of the Jerusalem congregation (cf. Acts 4:32-37) and the deceitful covetousness of a man named Ananias. During the beginning days of the early church, the Holy Spirit prompted many believers to sell property and houses to help support those within the church with special financial needs (Acts 4:34). (Note: They probably did not sell their primary dwellings [cf. Acts 4:37].)

    a. The generosity of Joseph (i.e., Barnabas [Acts 4:36]) and other believers must have evoked the approval of the apostles and gratitude from those in need. What did Ananias and his wife do with their piece of property (Acts 5:1-2)?

    b. Ananias' name means "whom God has graciously given" but he seems to have forgotten that. The name Sapphira comes from sapphire, a stone of exquisite beauty. How can we know for certain that their action was intentional, premeditated deceit rather than an innocent misunderstanding (Acts 5:2-3, 8)?

2. What did Peter tell Ananias about his rights to his own property (Acts 5:4)?

3. Some religious sects, such as Jehovah's Witnesses, do not believe that the Holy Spirit is an equal member of the Trinity. They believe that He is only a force or attribute of God the Father. What did the apostle Peter say to Ananias that refutes this doctrinal error that the Holy Spirit is not God (Acts 5:3, 4)?

4. Covetousness is a sinful attitude that causes an individual to desire strongly something that belongs to someone else. Since God continues to maintain sovereign ownership over all creation (cf. Ps. 24:1), a person can actually covet his own possessions because God has entrusted them only to his stewardship not his ownership. When he refuses to share those things that God has given him to help meet the needs of others, he is manifesting a covetous attitude.

    a. What things do you think Satan uses in our culture to influence people to covet?

    b. Most Christians are tempted to covet one particular thing more than others (e.g., a beautiful house or car, money, clothing, specific position or title, etc.). What one thing are you tempted to covet more than anything else?

    c. How do you protect yourself from this sin of covetousness?

5. There is a strong parallel between the sinful actions of Ananias and Sapphira and Achan, an OT Israelite who stole some of the spoil during the conquest of Jericho (cf. Jos. 7:1-26). In Achan's confession of his sin, Achan listed for Joshua three steps in his digression toward sin. Achan said first, **"I saw ..."**. Give the last two (Jos. 7:21).

6. Many American church leaders believe the church needs to become more accommodating to society in order to reach more people for Christ. As a result some churches have eliminated the kind of preaching that specifically addresses man's need for salvation and repentance.

    a. The apostles fearlessly proclaimed God's Word and even refused to obey the religious establishment's threats (cf. Acts 4:18). What were some initial responses to the early church's ministry (Acts 2:37; 4:1,-2, 13, 16; 5:11, 13, 17)?

    b. What were the results to this approach (Acts 2:41, 47; 4:4; 5:14)?

   c.   In what ways do you think the church in general can be more effective in our society?

7.   The apostles' preaching brought them into conflict again with the Jewish authorities (Acts 5:17 ff.). The Jewish high priest and his associates exercised their delegated political power by putting all the apostles in jail. Some Christians believe that the apostles were wrong for resisting the Jewish authorities because there is no authority apart from the ones appointed by God (Ro. 13:1). They believe the apostles faced God's chastening hand because of their rebellion rather than persecution (cf. Ro. 13:2). How can we be sure that the apostles were right to continue preaching the truth despite the Jewish authorities' forbidding them to do so (Acts 5:17-20)?

8.   After the angel opened the gates of the prison, the apostles entered the temple at daybreak and began to preach to the people (Acts 5:21). Again, the Jewish authorities had them arrested (cf. Acts 5:26, 27).

   a.   What did the Jewish leaders say to the apostles this time (Acts 5:28)?

   b.   What had the Jewish people (including the religious leaders) said to Pilate at the time of the crucifixion that made their present statement to the apostles seem so ridiculous (Matt. 27:24-25)?

   c.   What was Peter's response to their accusations (Acts 5:29-32)?

Read - Acts 5:1-6:7; other references as given.

Before you begin, take a moment to ask God to help you understand and apply the precious truths you will be learning. May God bless your study of His Word.

9.   The Jewish authorities became so enraged over Peter's and the apostles' unwillingness to compromise that they wanted to kill them (Acts 5:33).

    a.   Whom did God use to ease this tense situation and bring a resolution to the matter (Acts 5:34; 21:40-22:3)?

    b.   How did he resolve this tense situation so that no one was killed (Acts 5:34-41)?

10.   The apostles were flogged and released after they had been warned again not to speak in the name of Jesus (Acts 5:40).

    a.   How did they respond to this severe persecution (Acts 5:41-42)?

    b.   It has been said, "The only thing necessary for evil to prevail is for good men to do nothing." The apostles risked their lives to reach the people of Jerusalem, and God honored their faith as thousands were saved. What specific things are you doing to fulfill Christ's command to be His witness so that others can receive the gift of eternal life?

11. The early Jerusalem church was a model church, but it was not a perfect church. It was a model church because it continued to glorify God in spite of severe persecution and internal disruptions.

   a. The church's first internal problem (Ananias' attempted deception) was immediately resolved by God's direct intervention (Acts 5:1 ff.). What was the second internal problem that this infant church faced (Acts 6:1)?

   b. The word *neglected* (Gr. *paratheoreo* - to overlook, neglect) indicates that the oversight was not necessarily intentional. After becoming aware of the problem, the apostles attacked the problem, not the people who had been insensitive to the Greek-speaking Jewish widows (i.e., Hellenists). Although the apostles could have attempted to meet this need themselves, they believed that it was unwise for them to do so. What reason did they give for their actions (Acts 6:2, 4)?

   c. What do you think would have happened to the church if the apostles had attempted to meet this need themselves?

12. When the apostles instructed the congregation to select seven men to oversee this important ministry, they gave specific instructions regarding the qualifications of the men. Please list five qualifications of those who were to serve in this ministry (Acts 6:3-4).

13. How did the congregation respond to the apostles' recommendation (Acts 6:5-6)?

14. The apostles had to trust the Lord that the congregation would wisely choose qualified men to serve in this ministry. List several practical reasons it was better for the congregation rather than the apostles to choose these men?

15. Although the word *deacon* does not appear in this passage, many Bible scholars believe that the specialized ministry of these seven men became the progenitor of the future official office of the deacon-servant (cf. Phil. 1:1; 1 Tim. 3:8-10, 12, 13). Some Christian leaders have suggested that the spiritual character qualities listed in 1 Timothy should be interpreted as spiritual goals or objectives rather than essential spiritual prerequisites for a man to possess before he serves in this capacity. What proof does the Bible offer to show that these character qualities must be evident in a man's life before he is allowed to serve in this capacity (1 Tim. 3:1-2, 8)?

16. The early church faced persecution from religious authorities, hypocrisy, and a major threat to the unity and testimony of the church. At each crisis, the church trusted the Lord to meet their needs. What happened as a result of their latest effort to honor the Lord (Acts 6:7)?

Study # 4a   The Seed of the Church

Read - Acts 6:8-7:60; other references as given.

Church history has shown the truth of the ageless statement, "The blood of the saints is the seed of the church." Even today, thousands of faithful Christians give their lives every year for the cause of Christ.

In this lesson you will learn about the first Christian martyr, Stephen, and the grace that sustained him in his final hour of life – grace that will sustain you during your greatest trials. Before you begin, take a moment to ask God to help you understand and apply the precious truths you will be learning. May God bless your study of His Word.

1. Stephen was one of the seven men chosen to serve the widows so that the apostles could continue to pray and minister the Word of God (cf. Acts 6:5). According to the Bible, he was the first non-apostle to be greatly used by God and he became the first martyr of the church. How does the Bible describe this remarkable individual (Acts 6:3-5, 8, 10, 15; 7:59-60)?

2. God performed great wonders and signs among the people through Stephen (Acts 6:8). Most believers would like to be used of God in a great way. Stephen understood two important spiritual principles that every Christian must also understand before he can be greatly used of God. What are they (Mk. 10:42-44; Lu. 16:10-12)?

3. In Biblical times immigrant Jews often lived in close-knit quarters in Jerusalem and organized synagogues according to their ethnic backgrounds. The "Synagogue of the Freedmen" was probably not organized along ethnic lines but was likely comprised of former slaves and their descendants from North Africa (Cyrene and Alexandria) and Asia Minor. (Note: Asia and Cilicia were Roman provinces in what is now Turkey.) There are some interesting similarities between the way the Jewish libertines treated Stephen and the way the Jewish leaders treated Jesus Christ at the time of the crucifixion. What are they (Acts 6:11-14; Matt. 26:59-62)?

4. Many Christians believe that it is wrong to argue with a non-believer about Scripture because it only alienates the person from truth; however, Peter and the apostles

disputed the Jewish Council (cf. Acts 5:19, 29), and Stephen argued with the religious Jews. (Note: The Greek present participle indicates that the dispute continued for some time [Acts 4:4].)

a. If God commands Christians to be uncontentious and to refrain from arguing about spiritual matters (cf. Ph. 2:14; Titus 3:9-10), when, if ever, should a believer contend with another person about Biblical truth (Acts 15:1-2; Jude 1:3)?

b. What aspect of the Christian life should a believer never dispute or pass judgment on another believer (Ro. 14:1-5)?

c. Describe a situation when you disputed with another believer because you failed to understand the important distinction between universal fundamental truths and personal spiritual convictions.

5. In Stephen's address to the religious Jews (Acts 7:2-50), he reviewed Israel's history and the contributions made by Abraham (Acts 7:2-8), Joseph (Acts 7:9-17), Moses (Acts 7:20-44), Joshua (Acts 7:45), and David and Solomon (Acts 7:46-50). Stephen accused the Jewish leaders of utterly failing to comprehend God's plan for Israel in the past and the future. The Jews' failure to obey God was a direct result of their inability to see what God was doing on their behalf. The sermon begins the **"God of glory"** (Acts 7:2) and ends with Stephen seeing the **"glory of God"** (Acts 7:55).

a. Rather than glorifying God, the Jews venerated notable men such as Abraham and Moses through whom God had worked His sovereign will (cf. Jn. 8:53). As Stephen recounted Israel's history, he mentioned several things that God did for His people. What are they (Acts 7:2-8)?

b. Like the ancient Jews, some modern Christians fail to see God working in their lives. What specific things has God done recently to direct your life?

    c.   Why do you think Christians have difficulty recognizing God's working in their lives?

6.   God's sovereignty extends over all aspects of life. During the time of Joseph and the patriarchs, God's divine working on behalf of His people extended beyond His guidance of one man (i.e., Abraham). List five more evidences of God's provision and guidance during this time (Acts 7:9-17; cf. Gen. 37:18-38).

7.   Some believers seem almost irresistibly drawn to ministries that offer an endless diet of Bible messages that focus on what God can do for man (e.g., *The Four Easy Steps to Success* or *Five Easy Steps to Worry Free Living,* etc.). Rather than meditating on the person and attributes of God, they focus their spiritual attention on what God can do for them. While it is important for a Christian to receive practical instruction from the Bible, he must also learn to derive practical benefit from the deeper truths of God's Word.

    a.   How did Joseph's understanding of God's sovereignty practically affect his life (Gen. 50:15-21)?

    b.   How did the apostle Paul's understanding of God's sovereignty affect his life (Ph. 1:12-20)?

    c.   In what way(s) could a better understanding of God' sovereignty help you in your personal life, professional life, and future decisions?

Study # 4b   The Seed of the Church

Read - Acts 6:8-7:60; other references as given.

Before you begin, take a moment to ask God to help you understand and apply the precious truths you will be learning. May God bless your study of His Word.

8.   In Stephen's address he focused on God's divine power while almost casually mentioning man's weakness. Abraham's weakness was revealed in his inability to produce an heir (Acts 7:5). The patriarch's weakness was revealed in their treachery toward their brother Joseph (Acts 7:9).

   a.   How was human weakness revealed in Moses' life (Acts 7:20-24)?

   b.   What things didn't Moses understand about God's plan and effective spiritual leadership before he fled to Midian (Acts 7:24-28)?

9.   After Moses fled to Midian (Acts 7:29-30), he spent forty years raising a family and helping his father-in-law Jethro tend sheep (cf. Ex. 2:15-25). Although Moses believed that God wanted him to be a deliverer for His people (cf. Acts 7:25), he must have wondered if he had failed God and His people. However, God was using the normal routines of life to develop the godly character qualities that Moses would need for future ministry.

   a.   In what way(s) do you think Moses' time in Midian helped prepare him to be an effective spiritual leader?

   b.   In what way(s) do you think God might be using the normal routines of your life to prepare you for future ministry?

10. Stephen's review of Moses' life begins with God's appearance to him at the burning bush (vv. 30-35) and concludes with the miraculous deliverance of the Israelites from Egypt (vv. 36). He identifies Moses as a great spiritual leader and as a prophet of God. He quotes Moses' own words, **"The Lord your God will raise up for you a Prophet like me from your brethren"** (Acts 7:37), referring to Jesus Christ. Like Moses, Jesus delivered people from bondage to a heavy taskmaster (i.e., Satan). In what other ways were the lives and ministries of Moses and Jesus Christ similar (Ex. 2:3; Nu. 12:1; De. 34:5; Matt. 2:13; Mk. 16:1-6; Jn. 1:17; Jn. 7:3-6)?

11. At the time of the Exodus, the Israelites were delivered from physical death if they had the blood of the Passover lamb applied to their lintel and two doorposts of their homes (cf. Ex. 12:21-24). God offered them no other way to be rescued from that great peril. Are you absolutely sure that the blood of Jesus Christ has been applied to your sin (Jn. 14:6; Acts 4:12)?

12. How did the Israelites respond to this great prophet Moses who performed miracles in their midst and led them through the wilderness (Acts 7:39-41, 43)?

13. How did God respond to the Israelites' unwillingness to follow Him (Acts 7:42-45)?

14. God fulfilled His original promise to Abraham (i.e., a land of their own) even though the Jews consistently resisted His will (Acts 7:46-50). Both the Israelites' conquest of the Promised Land and Solomon's construction of the temple were a testimony to God's faithfulness rather than the Jews' godliness.

   a. How did Stephan apply his sermon to his listeners (Acts 7:51-53)?

   b. How did they respond to Stephen's sermon application (Acts 7:54, 57-60)?

15. Jesus Christ's last words on the cross, **"It is finished"** (Jn. 19:30) are a translation of a single Greek word, *tetelestai.* a term used for commercial purposes and similar to the English phrase, "paid in full." When Christ died on the cross, he paid man's sin debt in full. All those who are willing to accept His sacrifice as payment for their sins will be saved (cf. Ro. 10:13). Now Christ is seated at the right hand of the Father, signifying His finished work of redemption (cf. Mk. 16:19; Col. 3:1; Heb. 10:12).

    a. God allowed Stephen, the first Christian martyr, to see a rare vision of heaven just prior to his death. Describe what he saw (Acts 7:55-56).

    b. What do you think this vision of Christ signifies?

    c. Every year thousands of God's followers are martyred for their devotion to their Savior. What do you think the church can do to make the general public more aware of this great tragedy?

Study # 5a   Reaching the Rejected

Read – Acts 8:1-9:43; other references as given.

When Jesus commissioned His disciples with these words, **"you shall be witnesses to Me in Jerusalem, and in all Judea and Samaria, and to the end of the earth" (Acts 1:8)**, some of His disciples must have thought – Samaria? To all orthodox Jews, Samaria represented the dregs of society.

In this lesson you will learn about God's heart for those whom society casts aside and His expectation that they all receive full acceptance within the church. Before you begin, take a moment to ask God to help you understand and apply the precious truths you will be learning.

1. The gruesome murder of Stephen was attended by a young man named Saul (Acts 7:58; 8:1). He held the coats of Stephen's murderers, giving hearty approval and encouragement to those who threw the stones (Acts 8:1). Thirty years after Stephen's death, Saul (later known as Paul [cf. Acts 13:9]) had a vivid recollection of his part in the murder (cf. Acts 22:20). Yet, he told the Philippians that he was **"forgetting those things which are behind and reaching forward to those things which are ahead"** (Ph. 3:13). Sometimes Christians become confused about God's forgiveness, believing that God may not have forgiven them for a specific sin because they are unable to forget the sin.

   a. What do you think Paul meant by the statement **"forgetting those things which are behind"** if he was still able to remember it thirty years later (Ph. 3:13)?

   b. Sometimes believers say they know God has forgiven them but they cannot forgive themselves. When this happens, the believer fails to trust God and forfeits the peace and joy that God wants to give him. Is there a sin in your past for which you have not yet been able to accept God's complete forgiveness? What do you think God wants you to do with it (1 Jn. 1:9)?

2. The stoning of Stephen marked the beginning of **"a great persecution [arising] against the church which was at Jerusalem** (Acts 8:1). How did God use the wickedness of man (i.e., the persecution of His people) to accomplish His will (Acts 1:8; 8:1, 4)?

3. Simon, the sorcerer, is commonly known as Simon Magus in Christian history (Acts 8:9-25). The word "Magus" is derived from the Greek word for sorcerer (*magos*). Bible scholars had long questioned the genuineness of Simon's conversion even

though the Bible says he believed (Acts 8:13). Apparently Philip thought Simon had been saved, for he allowed him to be baptized and continue with him as he ministered (Acts 8:13). Sometimes Christians struggle with such severe doubts about their own salvation that they are ineffective in their service to God. The book of 1 John was written to help Christians gain complete assurance of their standing before God (1 Jn. 5:13). Please list four evidences of genuine conversion (1 Jn. 2:3; 3:14; 4:13; 5:4).

4. When the report of Philip's fruitful ministry reached the church in Jerusalem, they immediately sent the apostles, Peter and John, to Samaria (Acts 8:14).

    a. What did the two apostles do when they arrived (Acts 8:15-17)?

    b. Why do you think the Holy Spirit was withheld from the Samaritan believers until Peter and John arrived (Matt. 16:18-19; Jn. 4:9, 22)?

5. Racial tension between the Samaritans and the Jews had existed for more than seven hundred years. (Note: Hostility had been so severe that a border skirmish north of Jerusalem once resulted in the death of fourteen people.) Jews who traveled from Jerusalem to Galilee normally went up the Jordan Valley to avoid the threat of provocation. (Note: Further evidence of this racial hostility appeared during Jesus' trip through Samaria when <u>all</u> the disciples went into the Samaritan city of Sychar to buy food [cf. Jn. 4:8].) How do we know for sure that Peter and John fully accepted the Samaritans as part of the new church (Acts 8:25)?

6. Philip was a fearless preacher of righteousness and an obedient servant of God willing to leave a successful evangelistic outreach in Samaria and go toward Gaza, a barren area southeast of Jerusalem. There he met an Ethiopian eunuch returning from Jerusalem to his home in ancient Ethiopia (modern day Sudan), which was a journey of about 200 miles. As a God-fearing Gentile and eunuch, he would have been keenly aware that he was not fully accepted in the assembly of the Lord (cf. Dt. 23:1). It is likely that the book of Isaiah held a special interest to the Ethiopian eunuch. Even though his recent trip to Jerusalem would have reminded him of his exclusion from Judaism, he was probably knowledgeable of God's invitation of total

acceptance, **"Seek the** LORD **while He may be found, Call upon Him while He is near. Let the wicked forsake his way, and the unrighteous man his thoughts; Let him return to the** LORD**, and He will have mercy on him** (Isa. 55:6-7).

    a.   What other encouraging promises might the Ethiopian have read in Isaiah (Isa. 56:1-5)?

    b.   The Ethiopian asked Philip to help him understand Isaiah 53:7-8 (Acts 8:34). Whom did Philip identify as the subject of this OT passage (Acts 8:35)?

7.   It is easy for believers to misinterpret the Word of God by either spiritualizing passages of Scripture that should be taken literally or by failing to see the Bible (the OT in particular) as anything more than a manual on ethical training. When the former error occurs, the interpreter's imagination becomes the criteria for truth. When the latter error occurs, the centrality of the message of Christ is missed. What did Christ tell the two disciples on the road to Emmaus about the correct interpretation of the Old Testament (Lu. 24:27)?

8.   Philip preached Jesus Christ to the Ethiopian (Acts 8:35). The man turned to Christ and was saved. (Note: This is more than an assumption since the man was baptized upon his profession of faith.)

    a.   What did the Ethiopian want to do immediately after he had trusted Christ alone for eternal life (Acts 8:36)?

    b.   What was Philip's only prerequisite for baptism (Acts 8:37)?

9.   There is a great deal of misunderstanding related to the doctrine of baptism in the church today. Some religious groups teach that it is necessary for salvation (i.e., baptismal regeneration). Some believe it should be done by sprinkling water on an infant; others by pouring water over the head of a child or adult; still others believe it should be done by immersion after the person has trusted Christ for salvation. According to the Bible, what is the scriptural manner or mode of Christian baptism (Acts 8:38; Mk. 1:9-10; Jn. 3:23)?

Study # 5b   Reaching the Rejected

Read - Acts 8:1-9:43; other references as given.

Before you begin take a moment to ask God to help you understand and apply the precious truths you will be learning. May God bless your study of His Word.

10. God used the Jew's persecution of the early church to scatter the disciples and fulfill the Great Commission. While the gospel was spreading to Samaria (cf. 8:5-25), North Africa (Acts 8:26-39), and the eastern Mediterranean coast (Acts 8:40), Saul and the Jews were increasing their persecution of the church in Jerusalem (Acts 9:1, 2). How were the early Christians known at this time (Acts 9:2; cf. Acts 19:9; 22:4)?

11. The word **Way** (Heb. *derek*; Gr. *odos*) is used frequently in Scripture to refer to an individual's manner or pattern of living that results from the choices he makes. This metaphorical use of this word reminds us of the familiar saying that shows the progressive relationship between a person's thoughts and what he becomes: "Sow a thought, reap a habit; sow a habit, reap a lifestyle; sow a lifestyle, reap a life; sow a life, reap a destiny."

  a.   How does the Bible describe the way of those who reject God's way (Pro. 4:19; 12:15, 26; 13:15; 15:9)?

  b.   How does the Bible describe the way of those who follow God (Pro. 10:29, 12:28)?

12. Many people seem to have lost their way in life. Adrift in a sea of moral relativism, they seem to grope in darkness, looking for answers to life's important questions. What should a believer, who knows the way, tell other people about how to find the way through life (Jn. 14:6; Pro. 6:33)?

13. In Saul's question, **"Who are You, Lord?"** the translators capitalized the words **You** (you) and **Lord** to signify deity (Acts 9:5). The Greek word for **Lord** (*kurios*) can be translated Lord, lord, master or sir. When Paul asked this question, do you think he understood the true identity of this heavenly figure (i.e., Jesus Christ - Lord) or was he simply acknowledging an unidentifiable authority (Acts 9:4-5; 22:8)? Why?

14. Throughout Christ's earthly ministry, He regularly gave sight to the blind (cf. Matt. 11:4-5, 12:22). However, Jesus Christ removed sight from Saul whom He had chosen as a special instrument to proclaim the message of salvation to the Gentiles (Acts 9:8-9). Why do you think God allowed Saul to become blind for the three days surrounding his salvation (Acts 9:8-9; cf. Ph. 3:4-6)?

15. Paul had gone to Damascus to arrest Christians and bring them back to Jerusalem where they would be imprisoned and even killed (cf. Acts 9:2; 22:4). Interestingly, he was arrested by God who rescued him from penalty of death and gave him eternal life (Ro. 6:23).

    a. How did Paul regard his continuing relationship to the One who saved him from the penalty of death (Ro. 1:1; Eph. 3:1)?

    b. How a believer views his relationship to Christ has a tremendous bearing on the way he responds to the commands of God. For example, if a Christian views Jesus Christ simply as Savior, he will often resist Christ's authority over his daily life (e.g., goals, priorities, finances, etc.). How do you think a Christian should view Jesus Christ's authority in his life?

16. God spoke to a disciple named Ananias about Saul's conversion. (Note: This is obviously not the same Ananias who was slain by God for his deceit [cf. Acts 5:1-7].) The Lord told Ananias to minister to Saul and help him regain his sight (Acts 9:11-12). Why was Ananias so apprehensive about going to see Saul (Acts 9:13-14)?

17. Ananias responded to the Lord's command in spite of his fears (Acts 9:17-18). Faith in God is not the absence of fear or apprehension but the willingness to trust and obey God in spite of our fears and thoughts contrary to God's will. Faith is "letting God have the last word when our mind wants to resist His will for our lives."

    a. God appeared to Saul in a vision and told him that he had been chosen to bear His name before the Gentiles, kings and the sons of Israel (cf. Acts 9:15).

Years later, Paul stood before a king and told him that he had been obedient to this heavenly vision (Acts 26:20). List three important steps Saul took in his early spiritual life that helped him fulfill God's plan (Acts 9:18-21).

b. List three initial responses to Saul's preaching (Acts 9:20-25)?

18. Saul escaped from Damascus with the help of his disciples (Acts 9:25). He returned to Jerusalem and attempted to associate with the apostles, but **"they were all afraid of him, and did not believe that he was a disciple** (Acts 9:26). As soon as Saul found acceptance by the apostles, he spoke out boldly in the name of Jesus (Acts 9:28). The Jews sought to kill him, but he escaped again, this time to Caesarea and Tarsus (Acts 9:29-30). What additional blessings did the early church experience as a result of Saul's conversion and the continuing spread of the gospel (Acts 9:31)?

19. The fulfillment of the Great Commission required a team effort by the early church. The apostles prayed, ministered the Word and gave spiritual direction to the early church. Stephen, Philip and others assumed important leadership responsibilities within the church and met pressing physical needs. The congregation responded to the spiritual leadership and preached the Word of God wherever they went. The church overcame persecution (Acts 4), hypocrisy (Acts 5) and a divisive spirit (Acts 6). At the same time, the church also struggled to make the spiritual transition from OT Judaistic belief to the NT age of grace.

a. Which problem do you think the early church faced that posed the greatest threat to the work of God? Why?

b. What problem do you think is the greatest threat to the church of Jesus Christ today? Why?

20. Some Christians believe that the church's greatest hindrance to effective ministry is its inability to unshackle itself from the man-made religious traditions of the past. How do we know that the apostle Peter was able to make the difficult transition from his OT Judaistic beliefs to God's plan for the church age (Acts 9:43)?

Study # 6a   Call No Man Unclean

Read - Acts 10:1-48; other references as given.

Every nation struggles with the question of civil rights. India has its caste system, the Islamic nations suppress women and flourish prejudice – often in the name of God. Even the Christian church has struggled with a religious caste system based upon worldly power and position (cf. Ja. 2:1-6).

The Bible teaches that the ground is level at the foot of the cross. Everyone who comes to Christ in sincere faith, regardless of past failures, is acceptable to God. In this lesson you will learn how the early church struggled to understand this truth and what they learned about God in the process.

Before you begin, take a moment to ask God to help you understand and apply the precious truths you will be learning. May God bless your study of His Word.

1. The subject of Acts 10 is the salvation of a gentile military officer named Cornelius and his household. The importance of this event is highlighted by the detailed account of his conversion story and its effect upon the Jewish believers in Jerusalem in the following chapter (cf. Acts 11:1-18).

    a. Please give a brief description of Cornelius (Acts 10:1-4, 22, 31, 11:13-14).

    b. God answered Cornelius' prayer by sending the apostle Peter to preach the message of salvation to them. What did you notice about the timing of the answer to Cornelius' prayer?

2. A Roman legion of soldiers consisted of ten cohorts of approximately 600 men each when it was at full strength (Gr. *speira*). A cohort contained six centuries, each under the command of a centurion. The centurion Cornelius had command over a hundred soldiers within the Italian cohort. (Note: The Italian cohort was likely named after the original members of the group.) Why was the conversion of this one man and his household given such a prominent place in the book of Acts (cf. Acts 1:8; 11:1-4)?

3. Cornelius is described as **devout** (v. 2; Gr. *eusebes*) and **"a just man, one who fears God"** (v. 22). The term **"feared God"** is perhaps used as a technical term to indicate that Cornelius was not a full-fledged convert or proselyte to Judaism. He likely attended synagogue worship, acknowledged the God of Israel and complied with many Jewish customs. A man of power and political influence, Cornelius would not have been fully accepted into the Jewish community as a "proselyte of righteousness". If Cornelius was honored and respected by those who served him, why do you think he explained everything to his servants before he sent them to find Peter (Acts 10:7-8)?

4. Both Cornelius and Peter saw visions from God within twenty hours (cf. Act 10:3, 9). Cornelius understood the words of the angelic messenger sent to him (Acts 10:7, 8) but Peter was greatly perplexed at the vision he had seen (Acts 10:17).

    a. Why was the vision so disturbing to Peter (Acts 10:10-15; cf. Lev. 11:46-47)?

    b. Some Christians believe a vision from God would strengthen their faith. What other reactions did people experience who had a visitation from God (Jn. 12:27-29; Rev. 1:1, 17)?

    c. What did Jesus say about those who have never seen a visible manifestation of the risen Lord (Jn. 20:26-29)?

    d. What did Jesus say to the scribes and the Pharisees when they asked for a sign from Him (Matt. 12:38-39)?

5. God was working in Peter's and Cornelius' lives at the same time even though neither of them knew that God was working in the other person's heart. While certain aspects of their particular experience were unique, this situation teaches an important spiritual principle that can help Christians when they are prompted to witness for Christ. What is this important principle (cf. Jn. 16:7-11)?

6. Some Bible scholars believe that the conversion of Cornelius occurred approximately ten years after the beginning of the church at Pentecost. Peter's refusal to eat animals that were considered "ceremonially unclean" according to the Mosaic Law indicates his continuing adherence to Judaistic beliefs during this ten-year period.

   a. What else does it indicate (Mk. 7:14-23)?

   b. From where did Jesus say was the source of all uncleanness (Mk. 7:20-23)?

7. Jesus Christ's words regarding the true source of man's spiritual uncleanness has profound implications on the Christian's personal spiritual growth, the ministry of the local church and society in general. Secularists believe that man's problem is social - the various negative influences within the social order. They believe that if poverty, racial prejudice and a host of other social maladies could be eliminated, man's basic problems would disappear. Christians believe that man's problems are not social but rather a result of his own spiritual depravity and social decay is simply a by-product of his own spiritual depravity. While most believers are not confused about the source of man's problems (i.e., man's depravity in general), they are often confused about the solution to man's dilemma.

   a. What did Paul say about his own attempts to control his own spiritual uncleanness or sin by self-effort (Ro. 7:19-24)?

   b. What did Paul tell the Colossian believers about their attempts to control the sin nature by adhering to a strict external religious code (Col. 2:20-23)?

   c. The great evangelist D. L. Moody said, "I have never met a man that has caused me more trouble than myself." Do you agree with his statement? How could you apply this statement to yourself and your relationship with others?

Study # 6b   Call No Man Unclean

Read – Acts 10:1-48; other references as given.

Before you begin, take a moment to ask God to help you understand and apply the precious truths you will be learning. May God bless your study of His Word.

8. In marvelous timing coordinated by the hand of a sovereign God, Cornelius' servants were directed to the same home where Peter was staying shortly after he received the vision (Acts 10:17, 18). The Holy Spirit told Peter to go downstairs to meet the men (Acts 10:19, 20). Having traveled about thirty miles, Cornelius' servants were invited by Peter to spend the night before starting back to Caesarea on the following day (Acts 10:23).

    a. When Cornelius met Peter, he **fell down at his feet and worshiped** *him* (Acts 10:25). Why do you think Cornelius did this when the Bible says he feared God, and he would have known not to worship men?

    b. Peter's opening words to Cornelius, his relatives and his friends reveal that he only partially understood the meaning of the vision of the unclean animals. What was his initial understanding of the meaning of the vision (Acts 10:28-29)?

9. When Peter questioned Cornelius about why he had sent for him, Cornelius told him about the visitation of the angel (Acts 10:30-33).

    a. What did Cornelius say that proved he and the others were well prepared to receive what God wanted them to know (Acts 10:33)?

    b. What do you do to prepare yourself properly each week to receive the spiritual truths God wants to teach you through the teaching and preaching of His Word?

10. When Cornelius explained to Peter about the angelic visit and the reason for their assembly, Peter gained a fuller understanding of the exact meaning of the vision of the unclean animals (Acts 10:34-35).

   a. Previously Peter thought the vision meant that he should not call any man unholy or unclean (Acts 10:28). How did Peter's understanding change (Acts 10:34-35)?

   b. Peter's progressive enlightenment regarding the meaning of the vision teaches an important spiritual principle about how Christians grow in their understanding of God and His Word. What do you think it is?

11. Peter realized that God had divinely arranged his meeting with Cornelius and his friends and had prepared their hearts to receive the message of salvation through faith in Jesus Christ. Peter's statement, **"that word you know,"** indicates that he believed his audience was knowledgeable about the essential events of Christ's sacrifice (cf. Acts 10:37-38).

   a. Peter and the other apostles were given the responsibility of announcing two important truths to the world. What were they (Acts 10:42-43)?

   b. What occurred as Peter preached to Cornelius and his friends (Acts 10:44-46)?

12. The conversion of Cornelius and his friends was an important aspect in the fulfillment of the Great Commission given to the apostles (cf. Acts 1:8). The remainder of the book of Acts details the expansion of the church through the missionary efforts of the apostle Paul and his companions. Jesus Christ had given Peter **"the keys of the kingdom of heaven"** (cf. Matt. 16:17-19), and God had fulfilled His prophecy by using him to open the gospel to the Jews (Acts 2), endorse the work of God in the lives of the Samaritans (Acts 8), and preach to the Gentiles (Acts 10). In each situation, Peter was present when the various groups received the baptism of the Holy Spirit (cf. Acts 1:1-14; 8:14-15; 10:44).

a. How did the Jewish believers accompanying Peter react to the conversion of Cornelius and his friends (Acts 10:45)?

b. What did Peter command these new Gentile believers to do now that they were saved (Acts 10:47-48)?

13. The visible manifestation of the Holy Spirit's presence in the lives of these new believers caused some Christians to become confused. Some religious teachers believe that an individual is born again by trusting Christ alone for eternal life but he must also receive the baptism of the Spirit sometime after salvation. According to this teaching, baptism of the Spirit is accompanied by the "gift of tongues." (Note: Their understanding of the gift of tongues differs from the only Biblical definition explained in Acts 2:1-13).

a. According to this theological perspective, only certain believers have received the baptism of the Spirit. What does the Bible teach about being born again and the baptism of the Spirit (1 Cor. 12:13)?

b. What is also true if a person has not received the gift/baptism of the Holy Spirit (Ro. 8:9)?

Study # 7a   **Truth Versus Tradition**

Read - Acts 11:1-12:25; other references as given.

Peter's evangelistic encounter with Cornelius and his friends caused rejoicing in heaven and a real problem in the church in Jerusalem. *Gentiles in the church? What was Peter thinking?* Today, similar voices in the church can be heard, *"What was he thinking?" "Doesn't he know that we always …?".*

In this lesson you will learn how Peter's gracious words assuaged the judgmental believers in Jerusalem. You will learn how to minister to those who often confuse tradition with truth and try to supplant spiritual reality in religious rules. Before you begin, take a moment to ask God to help you understand and apply the precious truths you will be learning. May God bless your study of His Word.

1. The conversion of Cornelius and his friends must have caused a celebration in heaven but it caused a problem in the churches in Judea (Acts 11:1). The phrase **those of the circumcision** (Acts 11:2) is likely used in a restrictive sense to identify the Jewish believers in Judea who still believed that adherence to the Law of Moses was necessary (cf. Acts 15:5; Gal. 2:12).

    a. News of the conversion of Cornelius and his friends reached the Jewish believers in Judea before Peter arrived back in Jerusalem. The Jewish traditionalists contended with (Gr. *diakrino* – to contend, to judge, to make a distinction, to separate one's self in a hostile spirit) Peter, assuming he had done wrong before they heard his explanation. What did they think Peter had done wrong (Acts 11:1-3)?

    b. If Peter had become defensive toward these Jewish traditionalists, the Jerusalem church could have easily found itself embroiled in a major controversy that could have threatened the unity of the church and impaired its witness for Christ. What did Peter do to resolve the matter in a Christ-like manner (Acts 11:4-17)?

2. Disagreements between believers can often be resolved if God's people will respond in a Christ-like manner. Unfortunately, many believers make the same error as the Jewish traditionalists did by assuming the worst then attacking the one they think has failed.

    a.   How do you normally respond when you think a family member, fellow Christian, or a coworker has done wrong?

    b.   How do you normally react when someone has falsely accused you of wrongdoing?

    c.   How could you respond in a more Christ-like manner when you are falsely accused?

3.   Controversy between two people is often fueled by other people acting foolishly. Rather than helping the disputing parties look to God for wisdom and understanding, these people feed the controversy by taking sides and gossiping to others who are not a part of the solution. In Paul's letter to the Philippians, he addressed a problem between two Christian women whose inter-personal problem had become known in the church. List several wise things that Paul did to help these two women resolve their problem (Ph. 4:1-3).

4.   When Peter recounted the conversion of Cornelius and his friends to the Jewish traditionalists (Acts 11:4-17), he was very careful to include the vision and instruction from God (Acts 11:5-10) and the Holy Spirit's command (Acts 11:12). How did the Jewish traditionalists respond to Peter's thorough explanation (Acts 11:18)?

5.   Previously non-Jews had been converted to Christ when Philip preached in Samaria (cf. Acts 8:4-25) and when he led the Ethiopian eunuch to Christ (cf. Acts 8:26-39). Why do you think the Jewish traditionalists had a greater problem with this situation (i.e., Peter's going to Cornelius) when they did not seem to have a problem with the conversion of the Samaritans and the Ethiopian?

6. Beginning in Acts 11:19 the narrative reaches back to the persecution that resulted in the death of Stephen (cf. Acts 8:1-3). Acts 8:5-11:18 is a parenthetical section that provides the basic details of the missionary expansion to Samaria, North Africa, and the eastern Mediterranean coast. During this time Saul was saved and began his ministry.

    a. To what specific areas did God direct believers as a result of the early persecution of the church (Acts 11:19-20)? (Note: Examine a map so you can become familiar with the specific location of these places.)

    b. The persecution of the early church resulted in martyrdom and imprisonment (cf. Acts 9:1-2). How did God use this attack upon His people in a positive way (Acts 11:20-24)?

7. The beginning of the church in Antioch is significant because it became the center of missionary outreach throughout the remainder of the book of Acts. When the Jerusalem church heard the news about large numbers turning to the Lord in Antioch, they sent Barnabas to visit the church (cf. Acts 11:21, 24).

    a. Why was Barnabas a good choice to send to Antioch (Acts 11:23-26; cf. Acts 4:36)?

    b. The Bible says a **"great many people were added to the Lord"** (Acts 11:24). For an entire year Paul and Barnabas **"assembled with the church and taught a great many people"** (Act 11:26). Many believers wonder if reports of considerable numbers of people coming to the Lord are genuine. List three evidences that the conversion of these people in Antioch was genuine (Acts 11:26-30)?

Study # 7b   **Truth Versus Tradition**

Read - Acts 11:1-12:25; other references as given.

Before you begin, take a moment to ask God to help you understand and apply the precious truths you will be learning. May God bless your study of His Word.

8. The churches in Jerusalem and Antioch were effective in the areas of evangelism and discipleship. What do you think the modern church can do to be more effective in evangelism and in making disciples?

9. While many people were coming to Christ in Antioch, the church in Jerusalem continued to be persecuted (Acts 12:1) (Note: The phrase **"about that time"** refers back to the events of Acts 11.) Herod the king was Herod Agrippa I, the grandson of Herod the Great who attempted to kill Jesus as a baby (Matt. 2:1-18).

    a. What motivated Herod to persecute the church to the point of death (Acts 12:1-3)?

    b. It is easy for many Christians to become discouraged when they observe political figures motivated by their personal political advantage more than by principles of right and wrong. If God has called the church to make disciples of all nations rather than trying to save the world through political activism, what can Christians do to influence weak politicians to make wise decisions (1 Tim. 2:1-4)?

10. The martyrdom of James, the brother of John, was followed by the imprisonment of Peter (Acts 12:3, 4). It is likely that Herod remembered Peter's prior deliverance from prison (cf. Acts 5:19) because he had him arrested and delivered to four squads of soldiers (Acts 12:4). Undoubtedly Peter thought that Herod intended to kill him just as he had killed James. How do we know that Peter was trusting the Lord during this time (Acts 12:3-6)?

11. The church prayed fervently for Peter (Acts 12:5). Again, Peter was miraculously delivered from prison and death (Acts 12:7-11).

  a. What do you think the death of James and the deliverance of Peter teach us about prayer?

  b. What important lesson(s) do you think Peter's deliverance might have taught the believers gathered in Mary's house about the power of prayer (Acts 12:5, 12-16)?

12. Peter's escape from prison led Herod to discontinue his immediate attempts to persecute the church in Jerusalem. He left Jerusalem and traveled to Caesarea where he attempted to alleviate some political tension with the people of Tyre and Sidon (Acts 12:20). Herod had imposed a food embargo on these two Phoenician cities and they were desirous of winning him over so that he might remove the embargo.

  a. What did the Phoenicians say to flatter Herod when they saw him (Acts 12:21-22)?

  b. Herod Agrippa I was a nominal Jew, the king of a Jewish nation, who posed as a zealous proponent of Judaism. The shouts of the Phoenicians, **"The voice of a god and not of a man!"** (Acts 12:22), reveal that these pagan idolaters were attempting to deify Herod. What did Herod do to turn their attention to the one true God and prevent them from glorifying himself (Acts 12:21-23)?

  c. What happened to Herod as a result of his unwillingness to glorify God in this situation (Acts 12:23)?

13. Herod Agrippa I attempted to destroy the people of God, but God destroyed him. The Bible says, **"the word of God grew and multiplied"** (Acts 12:24). What do you think this means?

14. The early church faced external persecution (Acts 4), internal hypocrisy (Acts 5), disunity (Acts 6) and a struggle with traditionalism. Take a minute to reflect upon your study of the first twelve chapters of the book of Acts.

    a.   What do you think was the greatest obstacle to the early church? Why?

    b.   Although the advancement of the Word of God throughout this world is ultimately due to the sovereign will of a gracious God, He is pleased to use faithful servants who are willing to trust Him to the point of death. From a human perspective, what do you think was the key to the effectiveness of the early church?

Congratulations,

    You have just completed a challenging study of an important portion of God's Word. May your hunger for the Word of God increase so that you can honestly say every time you sit down to study His Word, **"Now, therefore, we are all present before God, to hear all the things commanded you by God"** (cf. Acts 10:33). May God greatly bless you as you diligently study His Word.

Study #1a   You Shall Be My Witnesses

1. a. "Lord, will You at this time restore the kingdom to Israel?"
   b. He told them to focus their attention on being His witnesses rather than wondering if the kingdom of God was going to be established here on earth. He also told them that they would not be able to tell the time or the season which the Father had determined for the official establishment of the kingdom of God.

2. a. 1. Peter and John said that they could not stop speaking about what they had seen or heard (Acts 4:20).
      2. Peter told Cornelius and his household that God had ordered them (i.e., the apostles) to preach to the people (Acts 10:42).
   b. Answers will vary, but it is a command to be obeyed.
   c. Answers will vary but could include the following:
      1. The believer should develop his social, family, and work-related contacts so that he can witness to them.
      2. The believer should be trained in evangelism so he can become an effective witness for Christ.
      3. He should determine to make witnessing as a way of life a top priority.

3. They would soon be baptized with the Holy Spirit. The Holy Spirit would give them power to be Christ's witnesses to the remotest parts of the earth.

4. 1. Christ will come back bodily (**"in like manner"** [Acts 1:11]).
   2. Christ will come back to the Mount of Olives (Zech 14:4) (Note: This refers to His arrival with His church.)
   3. Christ will come with clouds and every eye will see Him (Rev. 1:7).
   4. Christ will return as a conquering hero to establish His kingdom and rule as the Lord of Lords and the King of Kings (Rev. 19:11-19).

5. a. The phrase "with one accord" means that a group of believers are united in spirit as a result of each believer humbly submitting himself, his thinking, and his will to the person and plan of Christ as revealed through His Word. The phrase, **"of one mind with one"** means much more than unanimity, a congenial attitude, or mere capitulation to the consensus of a group. It means that each individual must be sensitive to the leading of the Holy Spirit and desires to glorify God rather than seeking to promote his own personal spiritual agenda.
   b. 1. He should examine his spiritual life in light of the Biblical teaching on this subject.
      2. He should sincerely confess his sin of having an independent spirit and accept God's forgiveness.
      3. He should pray that God would help him manifest a Christ-like attitude that promotes unity among other believers.

6.   Perhaps Judas hung himself (Matt. 27:5) and the rope or a tree limb broke (Acts 1:18). Judas fell headlong to his death, and his body was ruptured in the fall. This last problem could have happened after his death when the body was beginning to decompose. A field, later known a Hakeldama or Field of Blood, was purchased with the money that the priests had originally given Judas to betray Christ (Acts 1:18). A limited number of other possibilities could apply.

7.   a.   Peter and the rest of the apostles evaluated their present situation in light of Scripture. The principle can be stated as follows: Evaluate your present situation in light of God's Word and make sure you are where God wants you. If you find that you are not within God's present will, make the necessary changes before attempting to discern God's will for the future.
      b.   Peter and the rest of the apostles were able to determine God's will for their lives by taking their counsel from the revealed Word of God. The principle can be stated as follows: Seek to determine God's will for the future by examining the Scriptures to learn what God's Word (i.e., His commands, promises, principles) teaches about the particular situation. (Note: Some Christians make important decisions based upon non-biblical influences such as impressions, feelings, circumstances [i.e., fleece-casting], poor counsel etc., rather than seeking the wisdom of God as revealed through His Word.)
      c.   The apostles prayed and surrendered their wills to God. The principle can be stated as follows: When you are faced with choices that appear equal and nothing in Scripture precludes you from choosing either one, pray and totally surrender your will to God. The apostles' surrender was an act of humility that enabled them to be freed from personal desire that might have caused a lack of peace subsequent to their decision.

8.   The apostles did not second-guess God's will for their lives. The principle can be stated as follows: When you have done the first three steps and you have made your decision, trust God to lead you. Christians can experience assurance and peace regarding their decision if they approach the decision-making process according to the will of God and trust God to answer their prayers (cf. Pro. 3:5-6).

Study # 1b   You Shall Be My Witnesses

9.   1.   There was a noise from heaven like a rushing mighty wind and it filled the whole house where the disciples were sitting.
     2.   The disciples saw tongues as of fire resting on each other.
     3.   The disciples were all filled with the Holy Spirit and began to speak with other tongues or languages.

10. a. Biblical tongues was one of the visible manifestations of the baptism of the Holy Spirit. It was a gift from God (cf. Acts 2:17) to regenerated men, enabling them to speak in foreign languages that they did not know. This supernatural gift was given for the purpose of glorifying God (Acts 2:11).

   b. Three times (vv. 6, 8, 11). The repetition of this phrase emphasizes the fact that the apostles spoke human languages which were previously unknown to them but were understandable to the people present in Jerusalem at that time. (Note: The Greek word used for language "*dialektos,*" from which the English word dialect is derived, is the same word in verses six and eight).

11. 1. The accused should evaluate his own attitude to see whether he is able to defend his actions in a spirit of gentleness, and he is free from any hint of defensiveness or retaliation (Pro. 15:1).

   2. The accused should consider whether he really understands the perceived accusation before he responds (Pro. 18:23). Sometimes, a perceived accusation is nothing more than a poorly worded statement or question.

   3. The accused should consider the source (i.e., the emotional and spiritual condition of the one making the accusation, Pro. 26:4, 5). Some people will take any explanation of a person's actions as a further attempt to justify wrongdoing. Others, who are not so critical, will be helped by an explanation.

   4. The accused should consider whether he is defending his actions for God's glory or defending himself (1 Cor. 10:31).

12. a. Peter said that Jesus was a man who was authenticated (attested, Gr. *apodeiknimi* - to demonstrate, to prove by arguments, to exhibit) to the nation of Israel ("to you") by God by miracles, wonders, and signs which He (God) performed through Him (Christ). He said these miraculous signs occurred in their presence rather than in secret and proved that Jesus was the Christ.

   b. He said that Jesus was delivered up (i.e., to the Jewish leaders and the Roman authorities) by the predetermined plan of God. He said they (i.e., the Jewish people as a whole, the nation) were ultimately responsible for crucifying Christ even though the actual death of Jesus took place at the hands of the Roman authorities (i.e., godless men).

   c. Peter said that it was God's will for Christ to die even though wicked men carried out their own plan to execute the Savior. The theological balance must be carefully maintained so that both God's redemptive plan and man's sinfulness can be clearly seen.

   d. He said God raised up Christ, putting an end to the agony of death since it was impossible for Him to be held in its power. (Note: Christ had been raised before. The other raising of Christ was at the crucifixion (cf. Jn. 12:32). This proves that the manner of death of Christ was also a part of the predetermined plan of God.

13. 1. If there is no resurrection, not even Christ Himself has been raised (v. 13).
    2. If there is no resurrection, the message of Christ (i.e., victory over death through His resurrection) is empty and worthless (v. 14).
    3. If there is no resurrection, the Christian faith means nothing (**"your faith is also empty"** [v. 14]).
    4. If there is no resurrection, Christian servants who proclaim the message of Christ are false witnesses of God (v. 15).
    5. If there is no resurrection, the entire Christian faith is worthless (v. 17).
    6. If there is no resurrection, all men are still in their sins (v. 17).
    7. If there is no resurrection, those who have trusted Christ and are now dead, have perished (v. 18).
    8. If there is no resurrection, Christians who have falsely placed their total confidence in this doctrine, are the most deceived people on this earth (**"...all men the most pitiable"** [v. 19]).

14. Peter said that Jesus had been exalted to the right hand of God.

15. Jesus is now both Lord and Christ. (Note: The word "Lord" (Gr. *kyrios* - lord, master) refers to the exalted authority that the resurrected Jesus now possesses as a result of the Father's absolute endorsement. Proof that the early Christians meant to give Jesus the title "Lord" in this highest sense is indicated by their willingness to apply to Him several OT passages referring to Yahweh [cf. Joel 2:32]. The word "Christ" [Gr. *Christos* - anointed one] refers to the one chosen to be the OT prophetic messiah - the One chosen to be Emanuel, which means "God with us.")

16. a. They were convicted of their sin and said to Peter and the rest of the apostles, "Men and brethren, what shall we do?"
    b. Peter continued to encourage them to be saved and identify immediately with Jesus Christ in the waters of baptism.

17. a. 1. Biblical teaching through God-appointed spiritual leaders ("the apostles' doctrine").
      2. Christian fellowship.
      3. Worship ("the breaking of bread"). (Note: In the Greek Text, the definite article is present before the word bread, i.e., "the breaking of the bread." This means that it is likely a reference to the Lord's Supper, a significant worship event in the life of these new believers.)
      4. Congregational prayer.
    b. Answers will vary.

18. 1. The believers experienced a special sense of God's presence (**"Then fear came upon every soul"** [v. 43]).
    2. The believers experienced the continuing outpouring of God's power on the spiritual leaders of the new church (**"...many wonders and signs were done through the apostles"** [v. 43]).
    3. The believers experienced a strong desire for Christian fellowship that strengthened the bond and witness of the early church (**"And who believed were together"** [v. 44]).
    4. The believers experienced a spirit of generosity (**"...and had all things in common, and they sold their possessions and goods, and were divided them among all, as anyone had need"** [vv. 44-45]).
    5. The believers experienced a strong desire for genuine corporate worship and Christian fellowship (**"So continuing daily with one accord in the temple, and breaking bread from house to house, they ate their food with gladness and simplicity of heart"** [v. 46]).
    6. The believers experienced authentic, spontaneous worship (**"praising God and having favor with all the people"** [v. 47]).
    7. The believers experienced a spontaneous desire for evangelism and God's divine endorsement of their spiritual relationship with Him (**"And the Lord added to the church daily those who were being saved"** [v.47]).

Study # 2a   The Power of Jesus' Name

1. a. A lame beggar asked Peter and John to give him alms. (Note: The word "alms" [Gr. *eleemosune* - a gift for the poor] comes from the Greek root word *"eleos,"* which is usually translated mercy. God extends mercy to man by giving a gift to the spiritually poor - the gift of eternal life through Jesus Christ.)
   b. 1. The Law of Moses required the Israelites to provide for the needs of the poor among them (De. 15:7-11). Perhaps the lame beggar thought he would receive alms from the faithful ones who went to the temple to pray.
       2. The temple included large area and was often crowded (Acts 3:9).

2. 1. Christians should realize that poverty cannot be eliminated by Christian benevolence (Matt. 26:10-11). However, this does not mean that God's people should not help those in need.
    2. Christians should help meet the physical needs of the poor (Gal. 2:10). It is uncertain if Paul meant the poor in general or the needy believers whom Paul would meet as he conducted his missionary endeavors.
    3. Christians are supposed to do good to all men but especially to other believers (Gal. 6:10).

3. The healing of the lame man was a wonder or miracle because the man had been lame from birth (Acts 3:2). Apparently the man had a leg or ankle problem that prevented him from walking (Acts 3:7). It was a sign because it authenticated the ministry of the apostle Peter and also pointed others to Jesus Christ (Acts 3:6).

4. 1. They failed to realize that worshipping God under the New Covenant was not isolated to a specific place (Jn. 4:20-24).
   2. They failed to realize that the temple was not essential for the true worship of God because the Holy Spirit now lived within them and their bodies were the temple of God (1 Cor. 6:19).

5. a. Answers will vary.
   b. Answers will vary. Answers will vary but could include the following:
      1. Learn to recognize that not all change is wrong or an indication of compromise.
      2. Learn to analyze and evaluate opportunities for change from the perspective of God's Word rather than from the perspective of emotional comfort or cultural tradition.
      3. Learn to recognize change as a normal characteristic of spiritual life and as a potential opportunity for effective ministry.

6. a. 1. Peter said the healing of the lame beggar was not a result of their own power or piety (Acts 3:12).
      2. Peter said that God had glorified His Son and that the man had been healed on the basis of faith "in this name" (Acts 3:16). In Biblical times, a person's name meant more than a simple appellation – it was synonymous with the true nature and character of the individual. The phrase "In Jesus' name" connotes the full embodiment of the divine nature and authority of Jesus Christ. In Acts, Luke spoke of "the name" (Jesus or Lord) at least 33 times (cf. Acts 2:21, 38; 3:6, 16; 4:7, 10, 12, 17, 18, etc.).
   b. Answers will vary.

7. 1. The Jews disowned the Holy and Just One and demanded the release of a murderer (v. 14).
   2. The Jews killed the Author of Life, but God raised Him from the dead (v. 15).

8. a. Peter wanted the people to repent of their false understanding regarding the source of the lame beggar's healing. The man was healed by Christ, not man.
   b. Peter wanted the people to repent of their false understanding of the reason for Christ's death and suffering. He said the OT prophets had prophesied of the suffering of Christ, and His death was the fulfillment of their prophecies.
   c. Peter wanted the people to repent of their false understanding of the forgiveness of sin. It is likely that many of the Jews believed there was no way for them to atone for their sin of crucifying Christ. Peter told them that their sins (including the sin of killing Jesus Christ) could be wiped away. If they were willing to repent, the times of refreshing may come from the presence of

God. Some Bible scholars see this as God's offer to immediately establish His kingdom on earth.

9. Peter strengthened his call to repentance by proving that Jesus Christ was prophesied by Moses, Samuel and all the prophets and by identifying Christ as the promised seed of Abraham. Note: 1. Peter said the OT prophets told about the restoration of all things after Christ was received into heaven (v. 21). 2. He said that Moses prophesied about a future prophet God would raise up from among the people (v. 22). 3. He said that every soul who does not heed that prophet would be utterly destroyed (Acts 3:23). 4. He said that Samuel and all his successors announced the same thing: the coming of Christ (Acts 4:24). 5. He said that God had promised Abraham that "in His seed" (i.e., Christ [cf. Gal. 3:16]) all the families of the earth would be blessed [Acts 3:25]).

Study # 2b   The Power of Jesus' Name

10. a. 1. Some of the members of the religious council were members of the Sadducees, a religious sect that did not believe in the resurrection (Matt. 22:23).

    2. The Jewish authorities had fabricated a story that Jesus' disciples had stolen His body (Matt. 28:12-15). If the people believed in the resurrection, they would soon realize that the Jewish authorities lied about the disappearance of Christ's body.

    3. The resurrection of Jesus proved that God the Father had given complete endorsement to the life and person of Christ (Ro. 1:1-4).

    4. If Christ had indeed been resurrected, then Jesus possessed all the power of His divine office – a thought that would have been most unpleasant for the Jewish leaders to contemplate (Ro. 1:1-4).

    5. The Jewish authorities understood that the resurrection was the key to the Christian faith (1 Cor. 15:13-14). If there were no resurrection, then not even Christ had been raised.

   b. The religious leaders took Peter and John into custody and kept them in jail until the next morning (Acts 4:3). The next day they held a religious court with Annas, Caiaphas, and other individuals of high priestly descent in attendance (Acts 4:6). During this interrogation they asked Peter and John by whose authority the lame beggar had been healed (Acts 4:7).

11. a. Peter said the lame beggar was healed by the name (i.e., divine authority) of Jesus Christ the Nazarene, the One whom they crucified but God raised from the dead.

   b. The power of the Holy Spirit. Peter was filled with the Holy Spirit.

12. a.   To be filled with the Spirit means that the believer's thoughts, attitudes, and actions are under the complete control of the Holy Spirit who indwells him. He is trusting God and His Word rather than his own reason. Like a man who is under the influence of alcohol, the believer who is filled with the Spirit is under His influence.

   b.   Answers will vary.

13. **"Whether it is right in the sight of God to listen to you more than to God, you judge. For we cannot but speak the things which we have seen and heard."**

14. 1.   They were able to see their earthly struggles from a heavenly perspective by looking to God's Word rather than their own human reason (Acts 4:24-26).

   2.   They recognized that their persecution was the result of their identification with Jesus Christ (Acts 4:26).

   3.   They realized that God was sovereign and their persecution was part of His predestination for this world (Acts 4:28).

   4.   They turned their fears over to God in prayer, asking Him to give them boldness to be witnesses for Christ in the face of adversity (Acts 4:29).

15. 1.   A Christian will be able to live in complete spiritual unity with other believers (Acts 4:32).

   2.   A Christian will be released from a spirit of covetousness, seeing his material possessions as a tool to be used for God's service (Acts 4:32, 34-35).

   3.   A Christian will experience the grace and power of God in a more abundant way (Acts 4:33).

16. The early church faced a unique historical situation. Many of the people who were saved on the day of Pentecost were Jews and proselytes from different parts of the Roman Empire. They had come to Jerusalem for the Feast of Firstfruits (cf. Acts 2:5-13). Many of these religious pilgrims trusted Christ in response to Peter's preaching (Acts 2:41-42). Realizing the need for the apostles' teaching and fellowship, they stayed in Jerusalem but without an immediate means of financial support. It is safe to say that many unsaved Jewish antagonists would not be very willing to provide gainful employment to these new believers. Many Christians make the mistake of trying to reconstruct the NT culture. They forget that God has placed each generation of believers in a particular culture and has commissioned them to reach their world for Christ (cf. Matt. 5:13-15; Phil. 2:15). (Note: A major difference between Christian charity and communism is that communism is involuntary while Christian charity is voluntary.)

Study # 3a   The Church's First Hypocrites

1. a.   Ananias and Sapphira sold a piece of property and kept back some of the price for themselves and later brought the remainder of the money to the apostles.
    b.   Peter directly accused Ananias of lying to God by keeping back some of the price of the property (Acts 5:3). God's immediate judgment of Ananias confirmed the accuracy of Peter's accusation.

2. Peter told Ananias that the property was under his total control before he sold it, **"While it remained, was it not your own?"** Peter told Ananias the proceeds from the sale of the property also belonged to him, **"And after it was sold, was it not in your own control?"** Peter told Ananias that he was not forced to sell the property nor was he obligated to give any of the proceeds of the sale to the apostles. However, he was obligated to be honest with God.

3. Peter said Ananias lied to the Holy Spirit (Acts 5:3). Peter said that Ananias had not lied to men, but to God (Acts 5:3). The obvious parallel between these two verses is one of the clearest references in the Bible to prove the deity of the Holy Spirit.

4. a.   Advertising, fashion, human reason, love of money, peer pressure. Other answers could apply.
    b.   Answers will vary.
    c.   Answers will vary.

5. 1.   **"I coveted them."**
    2.   **"[I] took them."**

6. a.   1.   Those who heard Peter's message were convicted of their sin (**"cut to the heart"** [Acts 2:37]).
         2.   The Jewish priests, the captain of the temple guard, and the Sadducees were greatly disturbed (Acts 4:1-2).
         3.   The Jewish rulers, the elders, and the scribes marveled (Acts 4:13).
         4.   The Jewish leaders were confused and uncertain how to deal with the apostles (Acts 4:16).
         5.   Those who heard about the death of Ananias and Sapphira were fearful of God's judgment (Acts 5:11).
         6.   The general populace did not want to associate with the disciples (Acts 5:13).
         7.   The high priest and the Sadducees were filled with jealousy (Acts 5:17).
    b.   1.   Three thousand people were saved after Peter's message on the day of Pentecost (Acts 2:41).

2. More people were being saved daily so that the number of the men who were saved totaled about five thousand (Acts 2:47; 4:4).

3. Multitudes of men and women were saved (Acts 5:14).

c. Answers will vary.

7. An angel of the Lord released them from prison and said to them "Go, stand in the temple and speak to the people all the words of this life." (Acts 5:20).

8. a. "Did we not strictly command you not to teach in this name? And look, you have filled Jerusalem with your doctrine, and intend to bring this Man's blood on us."

b. "His blood be on us and on our children!"(Matt. 27:25).

c. Peter and the apostles said they must obey God rather than men (v. 29). The apostles also reminded the Jewish leaders that they were responsible for Jesus' death (**"The God of our fathers raised up Jesus whom you murdered by hanging on a tree"** [v. 30]). The apostles said God raised Jesus and made Him a Prince and a Savior, to grant (national) repentance to Israel and forgiveness of (individual) sins (v. 31). The apostles said they were able to testify to the accuracy of these things as well as the Holy Spirit whom God had given to those who obey Him (v. 32).

Study # 3b   The Church's First Hypocrites

9. a. God used a respected Pharisee named Gamaliel who was a teacher of the Law (Acts 5:34). He was a member of the Sanhedrin (the Council) and a mentor to the apostle Paul (Acts 22:3).

b. Gamaliel stood up in the Council and gave orders to have the apostles put outside so they could discuss the situation openly (Acts 5:34). He warned the members of the Council to be careful about their actions toward the apostles. He told them that the movement would come to nothing if it wasn't of God (Acts 5:35-38). On the other hand, if the movement was of God, they should leave the apostles alone so not to fight against God (Acts 5:39). The Council took his advice and released the men after they had flogged them (Acts 5:40).

10. a. They rejoiced that they had been counted worthy to suffer shame for Jesus' name (Acts 5:41). They kept teaching and preaching Jesus as the Christ (Acts 5:42).

b. Answers will vary.

11. a. The Greek-speaking Jewish widows who were living in Jerusalem were being overlooked in the daily serving of food. These were likely communal meals that the church provided at that time.

b. The apostles believed that they needed to commit themselves to prayer and the ministry of the Word. With so many new believers in the church, their time would be best spent praying for the church and teaching the new believers.

c. The new church could have experienced confusion and doctrinal error. This could easily have led to wide-scale discord and disunity within the church.

12. 1. The men must be from among the recognized congregation (**"among you"** [v. 3]).

2. The men must be believers (**"brethren"** [v. 3]).

3. The men must have a good reputation (v. 3).

4. The men must be characterized by the Holy Spirit's control in their lives (**"full of the Spirit"** [v. 3]).

5. The men must be characterized by practical wisdom (v. 3).

6. The men must possess administrative ability (**"we may appoint"** [v. 3]).

7. The men must be willing to work under the supervision of the spiritual leadership (**"we may appoint over this business"** [v. 3]).

8. The men must be willing to work independently so that the spiritual leaders can concentrate on their own spiritual responsibilities (v. 4).

13. The apostles' statement found approval from the congregation, and they selected seven qualified men (Acts 5:5). The congregation brought these men to the apostles for approval (Acts 5:6).

14. 1. The congregation would have been in a better position to know qualities of the men within the church.

2. The congregation's choosing the men would eliminate the potential accusation of apostolic favoritism.

3. The congregation's choosing the seven men would likely produce a representative cross section of the congregation.

4. The congregation might have been more willing to follow the leadership of men that they had chosen themselves. Other answers could apply.

15. The Bible says that a man who desires the office of an overseer (i.e., pastor or elder) must possess certain spiritual qualifications (1 Tim. 3:2). The phrase, "must be" is a translation of the Greek word "*dei*," which means "it is necessary" or "must be." Likewise, deacons must possess certain spiritual qualifications (1 Tim. 38 ff.). The word, "likewise" (v. 8), refers the reader back to the previous section of pastoral qualifications (cf. 1 Tim. 3:2 ff.). Just as the candidate for pastoral leadership must meet certain spiritual qualifications, the man who serves as a deacon must likewise possess certain spiritual qualifications before serving in this ministerial capacity.

16. The Word of God kept spreading, the number of the disciples continued to increase greatly in Jerusalem, and a great many of the priests were being saved.

Study # 4a   The Seed of the Church

1. 1. Stephen was a mature believer who had a good reputation (Acts 6:3).
    2. Stephen's life was characterized by godly wisdom and Holy Spirit control (Acts 6:3).
    3. Stephen was full of God's grace and power, and God used him to perform miracles and signs (Acts 6:8).
    4. He spoke out boldly for God (Acts 6:10).
    5. His face reflected the glory of the Lord (Acts 6:15).
    6. He was merciful toward those who killed him, praying that God would forgive their sin (Acts 7:59-60).

2. 1. A Christian must learn to be a servant of all people (Mk. 10:42-44).
    2. A Christian must be faithful in the "little" things that God has already asked him to do (Lu. 16:10-12).

3. 1. The two groups of Jewish leaders were unable to cope with the wisdom of Jesus and Stephen (Matt. 26:59-60; Acts 6:10).
    2. The two groups of Jewish leaders tried to induce wicked men to bring false testimony against Jesus and Stephen (Matt. 26:60-61; Acts 6:11).
    3. The two groups of Jewish leaders accused Jesus and Stephen of speaking against the temple (Acts 6:13; Matt. 26:61).

4. a. Christians should defend the fundamental truths (i.e., the faith) of the Bible.
    b. Christians should not argue with other believers about their personal convictions (Ro. 14:1-5).
    c. Answers will vary.

5. a. 1. God appeared to Abraham when he was still in Mesopotamia (Acts 7:2).
        2. God directed Abraham to leave his home and promised to direct him to a land that He would show him (Acts 7:3).
        3. God moved Abraham to Palestine as He promised (Acts 7:4).
        4. God reassured Abraham that He would give him and his offspring the land of Palestine as a possession (Acts 7:5).
        5. God told Abraham that his descendants would be enslaved in Egypt for four hundred years before He would bring them back into the land that He had originally promised Abraham (Acts 7:6-7).
        6. God gave Abraham the covenant of circumcision as a symbol of assurance that He would fulfill His Word (Acts 7:8).
    b. Answers will vary.
    c. 1. Many Christians are so preoccupied with the things of this world that they are unable to see what God is doing.
        2. God often works through providence (secondary causation; e.g., nature, etc.) to direct the affairs of life, so His working in the affairs of life is not easily seen.
        3. Other answers could apply.

6. 1. God allowed Joseph to be sold to Egypt, which allowed him to provide for his family at a future time (Acts 7:9).
    2. God allowed Joseph to experience His presence in a special way while he faced tremendous trials as a young person alone in a foreign land (Acts 7:9).
    3. God protected Joseph from all harm even though He allowed him to experience afflictions (Acts 7:10).
    4. God allowed Joseph to find favor in Pharaoh's eyes who made Joseph governor over all Egypt (Acts 7:10).
    5. God allowed a famine to occur in Egypt and Canaan. He used this famine to bring Jacob and his family to Egypt so they could fulfill His prophecy to Abraham (Acts 7:11-15).
    6. God allowed the Israelites to multiply, and He allowed another king (i.e., the Hyksos dynasty) to take control of Egypt who oppressed them. God used this oppression to motivate the Jews to cry out to God for a deliverer. God would use all these events to help fulfill His promise to Abraham (Acts 7:17).

7. a. Joseph was able to see the unfortunate events of his life (i.e., his brothers' plot to murder him, his enslavement and deportation to Egypt, the false accusation of Potipher's wife and his imprisonment, etc.) as a direct result of God's sovereign plan (Gen. 50:20). He was able to respond positively to every situation, using each "unfortunate" event as an opportunity to serve God. Joseph did not become bitter against his brothers, but was ready to minister to them (Gen. 50:21).
    b. Paul was able to see that his circumstances had worked out for the further progress of the gospel (Ph. 1:12). Paul's imprisonment (i.e., the positive way he responded to his circumstances) had encouraged other believers to share their faith with more boldness (Ph. 1:14-18). Their boldness had also been an encouragement to Paul (Ph. 1:18).
    c. Answers will vary.

Study # 4b   The Seed of the Church

8. a. Moses killed an Egyptian even though he experienced the favor of God (Acts 7:20), the motherly concern of Pharoah's daughter (Acts 7:21) and an excellent education (Acts 7:22).
    b. 1. He did not understand that there are two aspects to accomplishing God's will – God's work must be done God's way at God's time.
        2. He did not understand that effective leadership requires righteous behavior on behalf of the leader.

9. a. 1. Moses' time in Midian probably allowed him to gain the patience he needed to lead the Israelites.
        2. His time in Egypt allowed him to become accustomed to desert living, which would have helped him immensely as he led the people through the wilderness.

      3.   Moses' time in Midian probably taught him humility.

      4.   Moses' time in Midian gave him time to bond with his wife and help raise his two children before he devoted his attention to delivering the Israelites out of Egypt. Other answers could apply.

   b. Answers will vary.

10.   1. Evil men sought to kill both men at birth (Ex. 2:3; Matt. 2:13).

      2. Both men were raised in homes by at least one non-biological parent/guardian.

      3.   Both Moses and Jesus experienced resistance from within their immediate family (Nu. 12:1; Jn. 7:2-5).

      4. The exact location of their bodies after death was unknown for a period of time after their deaths (Dt. 34:5-6; Mk. 16:1-6).

11.   Answers will vary.

12.   1. The Israelites were unwilling to follow and turned back in their hearts to Egypt (Acts 7:39).

      2. The people asked Aaron to make idols to lead them (Acts 7:40-41).

      3. The Israelites took idols with them when they originally left Egypt (Acts 7:43).

13.   1. God judged that generation of Jews and gave them over to their idolatrous ways (Acts 7:42).

      2. God fulfilled His promise to bring Abraham's descendants into the land of Canaan (Acts 7:45). God worked through Joshua as He led the offspring of the Israelites who had perished in the wilderness.

14.   a. 1. Stephen told the Jewish listeners that they were just like their forefathers, stiff-necked and uncircumcised in heart (Acts 7:51).

         2. He said they were always resisting the Holy Spirit (Acts 7:51).

         3. He said their forefathers had killed all the prophets and they were now murderers and betrayers because they had killed the Righteous One (i.e., Jesus Christ).

         4. He said they believed angels had ordained the Law but they disobeyed (Acts 7:53).

   b. 1. The were convicted in their hearts because they knew Stephen's words were true (Acts 7:54).

         2. The began to gnash at him with their teeth (Acts 7:54).

         3. They cried out with loud voices and covered their ears so they could not hear what he was saying (Acts 7:57).

         4. They rushed upon him, seized him, and led him away to stone him to death (Acts 7:57-58). (Note: Stephen's statement regarding the spiritual condition of the Jews, **"You stiff-necked and uncircumcised in heart and ears! You always resist the Holy Spirit"** proved true even at his death.)

15. a. 1. Stephen saw the glory of God (Acts 7:55).
      2. Stephen saw the heavens open and the Son of Man (i.e., Jesus Christ) standing at the right hand of God (Acts 7:56).
   b. While it is impossible to be dogmatic, it is likely that Jesus' posture (i.e., standing) indicates His intense love and concern for followers who forsake their own lives to follow Him. With the exception of Christ's self-revelation to the apostle John (cf. Rev. 1:12-17), this is the only post-ascension reference to Jesus Christ in the Bible where He is not sitting. Since Christ's standing in the Book of Revelation likely indicates His readiness to judge the world, perhaps His standing at Stephen's death indicates His readiness to judge those who kill His servants. Perhaps Stephen understood Christ's actions this way and pleaded for mercy on their behalf.
   c. Christians need to be reminded that Jesus Christ is intensely concerned about all trials they experience as a result of their witness for Him. They need to be encouraged to stand up for Christ, knowing that He sees and appreciates their love for Him. Other answers could apply.

Study # 5a   Reaching the Rejected

1. a. Paul's statement, **"forgetting those things which are behind"** means he consciously and continuously acknowledged the sufficiency of Christ's sacrifice for his past sins whenever Satan attacked him. Paul did not allow his past failures to hinder his present devotion and obedience to Christ even though his sins were not removed from his memory. Rather than causing him spiritual defeat, Paul's past sins were a reminder of Christ's finished work on his behalf.
   b. Confess it and forget it. The believer should trust God and His Word rather than his feelings.

2. God used the persecution of the church in Jerusalem to scatter the believers throughout Judea and Samaria and fulfill Christ's commission to be His witnesses.

3. 1. A genuine believer will have the desire and power to be obedient to the commands of God (1 Jn. 2:3).
   2. A genuine believer will have a love for other Christians, manifested in a desire to fellowship and worship together with other Christians (1 Jn. 3:14).
   3. A genuine believer will have the Holy Spirit's internal witness giving him assurance regarding his relationship with God (1 Jn. 4:13).
   4. A genuine believer will be able to trust God for the things he needs in this life and for his eternal destiny (1 Jn. 5:4).

4. a. The two apostles prayed for the people to receive the Holy Spirit (Acts 8:15). Believing that God had answered their prayers, the two apostles laid their hands on the people, and they received the Holy Spirit (Acts 8:17).

    b.   The answer to this question must not overlook the particular social and historical situation of the day. The cultural rift between the Samaritans and the Jews could have greatly affected the unity and witness of the early church if the apostles had not been present to authenticate the genuineness of the Samaritans' salvation. The Samaritans needed to understand that salvation was of the Jews (cf. Jn. 4:9), and the Jewish believers needed to know that there was no partiality with God. By withholding the Spirit until Peter and John laid their hands on these Samaritan believers, God assured that the evangelistic work of Philip (a believer of Greek descent) was united with the work in Jerusalem. Peter's endorsement of the Samaritans' faith also fulfilled Christ's prophecy that gave Peter the privilege of introducing the message of Christ to the world (Matt. 16:18-19). Peter had already proclaimed the message of Christ's salvation to the Jews (Acts 2). Now he was given the privilege of sanctioning the opening of the gospel to the "half-Jew" (Acts 8). He would also introduce the gospel to the Gentiles when he preached to Cornelius and his household (Acts 10).

5.   Peter and John preached the gospel to many Samaritan villages as they returned to Jerusalem.

6.   a.   1.   The Ethiopian might have known God's promise to give foreigners full acceptance (Is. 56:3).

              2.   He might have also understood God's promise to give full acceptance to eunuchs (Is. 56:4-5).

    b.   Jesus Christ.

7.   Jesus told them that beginning in the Law (i.e., the first five Books of the OT) and the prophets, the Scriptures (OT) told things concerning Himself.

8.   a.   The Ethiopian eunuch wanted Philip to baptize him.

    b.   Philip told this new Ethiopian believer that he could be baptized if he believed with all his heart that Jesus Christ was the Son of God.

9.   Complete immersion in water of an individual who has trusted Christ alone for eternal life. Christian baptism should occur immediately after salvation, assuming the individual can testify of the personal saving work of Jesus Christ and the meaning of believer's baptism. (Note: The longest period of time between an individual's salvation and baptism was three days.)

Study # 5b   Reaching the Rejected

10. The Way.

11. a.   1.   Like darkness (Pro. 4:19)
          2.   Self-deceptive (Pro. 12:15)
          3.   It leads people astray (Pro. 12:26)
          4.   Hard (Pro. 13:15)
          5.   An abomination to the Lord (Pro. 15:9)
    b.   1.   A stronghold for the upright (Pro. 10:29)
          2.   Life (Pro. 12:28)

12.   1.   A believer should tell others that Jesus is the way (Jn. 14:6).
      2.   He should also tell other people that the commandments and teachings of God and the reproofs will help them understand the true way of life (Pro. 6:23).

13. He was simply acknowledging an unidentifiable authority. Jesus' answer to Saul's question proves that he was not sure who was speaking to him.

14. Answers will vary. Perhaps the Lord wanted Saul to understand his need for absolute dependence upon God. Since Saul was to be a chosen vessel for God, Saul needed to understand that he was dependent upon God for everything, including his eyesight.

15. a.   1.   A bondservant (Ro. 1:1).
          2.   An apostle (Ro. 1:1).
          3.   A prisoner of Jesus Christ (Eph. 3:1).
    b.   A Christian should view Jesus Christ as complete Lord and Master over all aspects of life. He should not look at Jesus Christ simply as his Savior but as the One who has absolute authority over his present life. Jesus Christ is the Lord and God's people owe Him everything.

16.   1.   Ananias had heard about the things that Saul had done to persecute the believers in Jerusalem (Acts 9:13).
      2.   Ananias had also heard that Saul had been given the authority from the chief priests at Jerusalem to imprison believers in Damascus (Acts 9:14).

17. a.   1.   He was baptized (v. 18).
          2.   He looked after his physical health (v. 19).
          3.   He participated in Christian fellowship (v. 19).
          4.   He immediately began to testify to others about the true identity of Jesus Christ (v. 21).
    b.   1.   All those who heard him were amazed (v. 21).

2. The Jews plotted together to kill him. (vv. 23-24).

3. Some people responded in faith and became "his disciples" (v. 25). This phrase does not mean that his disciples became rabid "followers of men" who were more concerned about what Saul believed than Jesus Christ (cf. 1 Cor. 1:10-15). It means that his preaching and teaching had been used by God to win converts to Jesus Christ who had tremendous spiritual confidence in Saul because of his loyalty to God.

18. 1. The church throughout all Judea and Galilee and Samaria enjoyed peace.

2. The church experienced a time of spiritual growth **"and were edified."**

3. The church continued to experience the fear of the Lord and the comfort of the Holy Spirit.

4. The church experienced numerical growth as well.

19. a. Answers will vary.

b. Answers will vary.

20. Peter stayed in Joppa with a tanner. An orthodox Jew would not intentionally expose himself to the possibility of contact with a dead animal because it would render him ceremonially unclean. This would be a violation of the OT Mosaic Law (cf. Lev. 11:39-40). The fact that Peter stayed at the home of Simon the tanner seems to indicate that he was beginning to question his continued obligation to the Mosaic Law.

Study # 6a   Call No Man Unclean

1. a. Cornelius was a Roman centurion within the Italian cohort who was stationed at Caesarea (Acts 10:1). He was a devout man who feared God, prayed continually, and led his family to a similar devotion of God even though he was not saved (Acts 10:2-4; 11:14). He was a generous man who gave alms to the Jewish people, and God was merciful to him by allowing him to see a vision of an angel of God (Acts 10:4).

b. God heard Cornelius' prayer before he was saved (Acts 10:31; 11:14).

2. 1. The conversion of the Gentile Cornelius fulfilled the commission that Jesus Christ gave to Peter.

2. The conversion of Cornelius and his friends revealed the tremendous struggle that the early Jewish church faced as they wrestled with the question of Gentile inclusion into the church (Acts 11:1-4).

3. It is likely that Cornelius wanted his servants to know what God had shown him in the vision so that they did not credit him with the success of their mission. The believer's ultimate purpose in life is to bring glory to God, and Christians should make sure that He receives the glory for what He accomplishes through their lives.

4. a. Peter was an orthodox Jew who continued to adhere to the OT Mosaic Law's dietary regulations . The vision of God that he received in Joppa instructed him to eat unclean animals, a direct violation of the Mosaic Law (Lev. 11:46-47).

    b. 1. God spoke from heaven but the multitude that heard the sound thought it was thunder (Jn. 12:27-29).

        2. When the apostle John saw the resurrected Lord Jesus, he fell at His feet as a dead man (Rev. 1:17).

    c. **"Blessed are those who have not seen and yet have believed"** (Jn 20:29).

    d. **"An evil and adulterous generation seeks after a sign"** (Matt.12:39).

5. At the same time as God is convicting the unsaved of their need for Christ, He is prompting the believer to share the message of salvation. Regardless of the results of verbal witness, the believer needs to trust God and speak when prompted by the Holy Spirit.

6. a. Peter did not understand that Jesus Christ had declared all foods clean (Mk. 7:19). The OT dietary laws ended with the beginning of the New Covenant. It also indicates that Peter did not fully understand the real source of man's moral defilement.

    b. Christ said that all evil proceeds from within, out of the heart of man (Mk. 7:21).

7. a. Paul said his own attempts to control his sin nature were utterly ineffective. He said that he found himself doing things that he did not want to do and not doing the things that he wanted to do (Ro. 8:19). He said that he was a prisoner to the law of sin (Ro. 8:23). He also realized that no philosophy or self-determination could rescue him from his problem, **"Who will deliver me from this body of death?"**.

    b. Paul told the Colossians that submitting to a man-made list of religious regulations will give the appearance of religious devotion but will not help them control the appetites of the sin nature. He said this approach appears to be wise but is of no value against fleshly indulgence.

    c. Answers will vary.

Study # 6b   Call No Man Unclean

8   a.   The word worship (Gr. *proskuneo* - worship, pay homage, make obeisance) is used in the NT to describe an individual kneeling or prostrating himself before God, Jesus Christ, heavenly beings, or demons. Cornelius was showing Peter the ultimate expression of eastern respect by falling prostrate before him but he was not worshipping him as God .

     b.   Peter thought that the vision of the unclean animals was given to teach him that he should not call any man unholy or unclean (Acts 10:28). At this point in his understanding, Peter still did not understand that God wanted the Gentiles to be fully accepted into the church.

9.   a.   1.   Cornelius said that he had sent for Peter "immediately," which shows his urgency to hear the message.

          2.   Cornelius said that they were "all present," which indicates the group's willingness to set aside other responsibilities to hear the message.

          3.   Cornelius said they were all present "before God," which indicates that they were willing to accept Peter's message as the Word of God rather than the words of men (cf. 1 Thess. 2:13).

          4.   Cornelius said they were assembled to hear "all" that Peter had to say, not just the things they wanted to hear.

          5.   Cornelius said that he realized Peter words came from the Lord. This meant that Cornelius and the others were willing to accept Peter's message as a divine command to be obeyed rather than a presentation of spiritual facts to be considered.

     b.   Answers will vary.

10. a.   Peter came to the understanding that God is not partial to a particular nationality. He also understood that God accepts anyone who fears Him and does what is right. (Note: This verse does not teach "works salvation" because a person's first responsibility before God is to fear Him, which is tantamount to trusting Him for eternal life and revering Him by a life of obedience.)

     b.   God often reveals spiritual truths to His people incrementally rather than in a series of dynamic revelations. Like the layers of an onion that can be removed one layer at a time, God often reveals spiritual truths to believers progressively. Understanding this spiritual principle will enable Christians to remain teachable when God provides further understanding to a spiritual truth only partially comprehended.

11. a.   1.   God has appointed Jesus Christ as judge of the living and the dead (Acts 10:42).

          2.   Everyone who believes in Him receives remission of sins (Acts 10:43).

b.   The Holy Spirit fell upon all those who were listening to Peter's message and they began to speak with tongues and exalt God (Acts 10:44, 46).

12. a.   The Jewish believers accompanying Peter were amazed at what they saw because they realized that the giving of the Holy Spirit meant God had fully accepted the Gentiles into the church (Acts 10:45).

b.   Peter commanded these new Gentile believers to be baptized in the name of Jesus Christ.

13. a.   The Bible teaches that every person who has been saved has received the baptism of the Spirit. The emphasis in this verse, **"all baptized," "have all been made,"** indicates that every believer has been baptized into the Spirit. There are no exceptions.

b.   He is not saved.

Study # 7a   Truth Versus Tradition

1.   a.   The Jewish traditionalists thought Peter had failed to obey the dietary laws of the Mosaic covenant by eating with Gentiles (i.e., uncircumcised men).

b.   Peter remained calm and proceeded to explain everything that had happened to him in an orderly sequence (Acts 11:4). His explanation included the vision of the clean and unclean animals (Acts 11:5-9), the Lord's command to kill and eat (Acts 11:7), the Lord's re-instruction to Peter (Acts 11:9), the Spirit's command to go with the men whom Cornelius had sent (Acts 11:12), the account of the angelic visitation to Cornelius (Acts 11:13-14), the previous words of the Lord regarding baptism in the Holy Spirit (Acts 11:16), and his own interpretation of the events (Acts 11:17-18).

2.   a.   Answers will vary.
     b.   Answers will vary.
     c.   Answers will vary.

3.   1.   Paul did not take sides.
     2.   Paul attempted to focus both women on the Lord (**"be in the same mind in the Lord"**).
     3.   Paul attempted to focus their attention on their future responsibilities rather than on their past or present failures.
     4.   Paul reminded both the Philippian church and the two women of their previous Christian service they had rendered to the Lord.
     5.   Paul solicited the spiritual assistance of a faithful member of the Philippian church to serve as a mediator between the two combatants.
     6.   Paul did not magnify the problem by dwelling on it more than necessary. Other answers could apply.

4. They accepted Peter's explanation and agreed that God granted the Gentiles the repentance that leads to eternal life.

5. Cornelius and his friends were the first completely Gentile converts whose salvation became known to the church in Jerusalem. Jerusalem believers accepted Samaritans' conversions because Samaritans were half-blooded Jews. When the Ethiopian eunuch was converted on his way to Africa, neither Philip nor the Ethiopian returned to Jerusalem, so the believers in Jerusalem might not have known of his conversion. The conversion of a Roman centurion and his friends would have become public knowledge, so the Jewish believers in Jerusalem felt they needed to reject or endorse the event.

6. a. Phoenicia, Cyprus, and Antioch.
    b. Some of the believers who had been persecuted in Jerusalem went to Phoenicia, Cyprus, and Antioch, preaching the Word to the Jews alone (Acts 11:19). Some originally went to Cyprus then traveled to Antioch from Cyrene and began preaching to the Gentiles (Greeks) also. The Lord used their preaching, and a large number of the people of Antioch believed (Acts 11:21).

7. a. Barnabas was a good man, full of the Holy Spirit and faith (Acts 11:24). He had already been recognized as a believer who was able to encourage other believers in the things of the Lord (Acts 4:36).
    b. 1. These new believers became disciples of Christ (Acts 11:26).
       2. These disciples were called Christians, which means the "party of Christ" (Acts 11:26). The name Christian was probably given to the disciples of Christ by the unsaved Gentile community who recognized that their attitudes and actions resembled that of Jesus Christ.
       3. They gave financially to the needs of the brethren in Judea (Acts 11:29).

Study # 7b   Truth Versus Tradition

8. Answers will vary.

9. a. Herod Agrippa wanted to please the Jews (Acts 12:3).
    b. Pray that God will help them make wise decisions (1 Tim. 2:1-2).

10. Peter was sleeping on the night before Herod intended to kill him (Acts 12:6).

11. a. God's people have no guarantee that all their prayers for the physical deliverance of others will be answered. Undoubtedly, the church was praying for James' deliverance from death just as they were praying for Peter. God's unwillingness to answer some of the prayers of His people indicates that He

often has a higher purpose than the preservation of human life, even the lives of His people.

    b.   1.   A believer can pray fervently while still not believing that God will answer his prayers.

           2.   A believer might believe that God is answering his prayer when, in reality, God might be accomplishing His will independent of a believer's faithless prayer. Other answers could apply.

12. a.   **"The voice of a god and not of a man"** (Acts 12:22).

      b.   Nothing.

      c.   The Lord struck him for not giving God the glory, and he was eaten by worms and died (Acts 12:23).

13. The truth of God continued to be accepted by people as they were saved and continued to grow. The Word of God multiplied as those who accepted the Word shared it with others who also accepted it.

14. a.   Answers will vary.

      b.   Answers will vary.